THE POLITICS OF THE FORKED TONGUE

Authoritarian Liberalism

Published in the United Kingdom in 2002 by

New European Publications Limited
14-16 Carroun Road
London SW8 1JT, England

British Library Cataloguing in Publication Data

ISBN   1-8724-1016-2

Cover and page layout   www.orbitgraphic.co.uk

Composed in Bell Centennial & Minion
Printed and bound in Great Britain by Antony Rowe, Chippenham, Wiltshire.

THE POLITICS OF THE FORKED TONGUE

Authoritarian Liberalism

Aidan Rankin

NEW EUROPEAN PUBLICATIONS LONDON

For my Mother and Father,
Anne and David Rankin,
With love and gratitude.

He who would do good to another must do so in
Minute Particulars. General Good is the plea of the
scoundrel, hypocrite and flatterer.

William Blake

Foreword

by John Coleman

One of the most important things in life, I believe, is not to jump to conclusions. The essence of the scientific spirit is to keep an open mind for as long as is reasonably possible. Darwin's story about playing the trumpet to the tulips in his garden once a year in order to keep his mind open to the possibility of the unexpected is a wonderful example of the true scientific spirit and contrast rather disturbingly with the scientific fundamentalism of the modern age. Postmodernism is also subject to a similar danger if it jumps to conclusions that lead it to cast off both the best of traditional thought and serious scientific analysis without adequate consideration.

One of the most dangerous tasks any writer can undertake is to challenge those ideas which unconsciously shape the direction of the society in which he has to live and work. A remark attributed to Sigmund Freud when he arrived in England just before the Second World War comes to mind. He could, he said, do what he liked and say what he liked in England, and he added: 'I almost said think what I like'. Every age has its censor just below the level of ordinary consciousness, protecting the ideas which it senses are the very basis of its *modus operandi*. In a graphic piece from T.E. Hulme's *Notebook*, which appeared in *The New Age* in 1916, he wrote:

> In order to understand a period it is necessary not so much to be acquainted with its more defined opinions as with the doctrines which are thought of not as doctrines but as **facts**. (The moderns, for example, do not look for their belief in progress as an opinion, but merely as a recognition of fact.) There are certain doctrines which for a particular period seem not doctrines but inevitable categories of the human mind. Men do not look on them much as correct opinions, for they have become so much part of the human mind, and lie so far back, that they have never really been conscious of them at all. They do not see them, but other things through them.

Aidan Rankin is arguing that a process of this sort is taking place today through the various brands of political correctness and that although this is more obvious in American society than it is in Britain or continental Europe, perhaps for that very reason it is more dangerous here. It would be easy in a superficial way to say that he is trying to read too much into our post-modern way of thinking. But is he? People sometimes say to me: 'PC is only a passing fad'. Rankin is arguing that it is something much more fundamental that affects our legal system, our political ideas, our employment practices and above all our moral decisions. A couple of examples may illustrate it. The wife of a chef running a restaurant in Hampshire was talking to me about bringing up her children when they were young instead of going out to work. It was the happiest period of her life, she said, and after slight hesitation added, 'but I suppose I'm not meant to think that today'. Doris Lessing made another interesting comment on this form of internalised censorship:

> The most stupid, ill-educated and nasty woman can rubbish the nicest, kindest and most intelligent man and no one protests.

Wise men have always advised us to be on our guard against tyranny, which usually comes in the first place wrapped in good intentions. Burke, for example, said that all that was necessary for evil to triumph is for good men to do nothing. As long ago as 63BC, Julius Caesar warned the Senate about the dangers of the thin end of the wedge:

> The Lacedaemonians, when they had conquered the Athenians, placed thirty governors over them; who began their power by putting to death, without any trial, such as were remarkably wicked and universally hated. The people were highly pleased at this, and applauded the justice of such executions. But when they had by degrees established their lawless authority, they wantonly butchered both good and bad without distinction; and thus kept the State in awe. Such was the severe punishment which the people, oppressed with slavery, suffered for their foolish joy.

Although the subject matter might appear much less serious than that which Caesar described, it is still important to keep an open mind when reading through the chapters of Rankin's analysis and to find reassurance in his 'Afterword', perhaps especially in his quotation from George Orwell. Rankin wants to hold on to not only the best in the conservative tradition but the best in the socialist tradition also. He believes in the importance of John Stuart Mill's clash between truth and falsehood, which in the end leads the more sophisticated of us to nothing more than a little good sense which simple, honest people have usually arrived at directly through the ages.

Preface

This is, I fear, another book about 'political correctness'. I am aware that much has been written already about the comic and annoying aspects of this curious cultural phenomenon. I am aware, too, that many solemn tomes, magazine features and newspaper column inches have been devoted to the threats to freedom and responsibility that the 'politically correct' mentality might pose. Political correctness has been defined variously. It has been described as a series of pious linguistic strictures, such as being told to say 'firefighter', 'chair' or 'coffee without milk'. It has been associated, in the right-wing press especially, with the attack on 'traditional' families and communities, through the 'promotion of homosexuality' and the breakdown of heterosexual marriage. It is seen as the motive behind attempts to erase the past, good and bad, in the name of a multicultural ideal. At the same time that it is attacked, it is loudly and somewhat desperately defended by liberals, who do not use the phrase political correctness, but employ the more traditional language of human rights and social justice, ideas that underpin our notions of freedom and fairness.

That political correctness should mean 'all things to all people' is a sign of the complexity of the phenomenon. For it is not, as some conservatives suggest, a threat to Western civilisation, being itself entirely a product of Western thought. Nor is it, as some on the left imply, a myth or label invented by reactionaries to discredit attempts to build a more inclusive society. Nor should our critique of PC be limited to anecdotes and one-liners, although it is healthy and right that we should laugh at its excesses. One of the characteristics of political correctness is that its adherents see every aspect of life as 'political' and draw no distinction between private and public spheres. Their strictures apply equally to large-scale projects, such as European political union or the elusive 'global governance', and apparently minor details such as the words we use or the jokes we tell. This 'politicisation of everything' helps to explain the blend of pettiness and grandiloquence that characterises the PC mentality. The censorious nature of political correctness, and its American origins, makes it tempting to see the phenomenon as a new type of Puritanism. There are, after all, many aspects of PC that resemble Protestant fundamentalism: proscriptive 'speech codes', a belief in atonement for past sins and a sense of moral crusade that can override practical politics. Yet even this view of political correctness is a caricature. For although it has a strong Puritanical streak – and is arguably a form of secular fundamentalism – it is also very much the offspring of the late twentieth century New Left. Its chief exponents are radicals who have seen their dreams of an egalitarian economic order destroyed and so lead lives of noisy desperation. Their shift of emphasis from social and economic change to an identity politics based on race, sex and sexual orientation is in many ways a sign of pessimism, not hope for the future. Their obsessions with 'anti-racism', feminism and gay rights are expressed with passionate intensity and, in many cases, virulent hatred. This is because such causes represent the threadbare remains of a much wider and more generous social vision.

We can, I believe, make sense of the PC phenomenon in terms of two political and cultural changes, one in liberalism, and the other on the Left, whether Marxist or 'post-Marxist'. In liberalism, there has been a shift of emphasis from preserving (and sometimes building upon) traditional liberties to codifying and enshrining new 'rights'. Simultaneously, the emphasis of liberal political thought has shifted from the individual – and the concept of individual freedom under the rule of law – towards the collective. Thus the new liberal divides the population into groups and assigns them group rights, rather than treating them as autonomous individuals with their own needs. This change in liberal thought has been accompanied by a change on the Left that was evolving anyway but has been precipitated by world events. As liberals moved away from individualism in the social and political spheres, the Left moved away from collectivist economics, in extreme cases embracing the fashionable 'market forces' cargo cult with the zeal of the converted. To compensate for this change, the Left turned its attention relentlessly to cultural matters. It abandoned, for the most part, the motif of class struggle, replacing it with new conflicts – between black and white, women and men, homosexuals and heterosexuals. All these struggles preserved the familiar idea of opposing forces, one representing progress, the other reaction, one 'saved', the other eternally 'damned'. They preserved the idea of radical social change, but projected it towards the social and intimate spheres, hence the popular New Left slogan; 'the personal is political'. Above all, the rise of identity politics, as it quickly became known, continued the idea that the group or category is more important than the individuals who comprise it.

The Left's large-scale abandonment of common ownership as an ideal, and the liberal shift of emphasis from individuals to groups has made for an ideological convergence between these 'progressive' political forces, based around identity politics and group rights. The result has been an authoritarian variant of liberalism that still uses the language of freedom, but calls for a massive amount of state intervention on behalf of 'oppressed groups' – whether members of those groups wish it or not. Meanwhile, the Left still uses the language of equality but applies it to questions of race and sexuality instead of distribution of wealth or ownership of the 'means of production'.

The result of all this is the potent but confused social agenda that we refer to as political correctness. I have called it the politics of the forked tongue because it appears to point in two directions simultaneously. At one level, its rallying cry is the inclusive society, whereby differences of ethnicity, 'gender' or sexual preference count for nothing and traditional loyalties to nation, class or even locality dissolve into the ether. At another level, identity politics attempts to balkanise the population along racial or sexual lines.

This is why we have professed 'anti-racists', usually white as it happens, whose campaigns are based entirely on classifying individuals by their ethnic origins. 'Anti-fascists' advocate censorship and try to stifle other opinions by intimidation and force – the classic techniques of fascism itself. We also have feminists who, in the name of women's rights, insist that all women undertake paid employment and condemn those who wish to be full-time mothers. In their rigidity and their obsession with work and career, they imitate the worst of 'male' values. They call to mind the self-destructive ambitions of Lady Macbeth, who called on divine powers to 'unsex me here'. But just as most 'anti-racist' campaigners are white, so many radical feminists are men. Likewise the homosexual movement depends for its survival on the support of 'liberal' heterosexuals. They find this movement's slogans comforting, because they allow them to express 'solidarity' without having to think much about a topic they find uncomfortable.

Forked-tongued politics has created a *nomenklatura* of single-issue activists and bureaucrats. They attack not only their perceived opponents, but often direct their strongest ire at members of 'their' constituencies. Thus 'anti-racists' accuse black opponents of race treachery, feminists denigrate and abuse women who oppose them and gay activists use threats and moral blackmail against homosexuals who do not share their aims. Authoritarian liberalism devalues representative democracy, in which people vote as individual citizens, and elevates unrepresentative pressure groups, whose activists are accountable to nobody but claim to speak for millions.

When I began to research political correctness, it was from the standpoint of cultural – as opposed to political – conservatism. After all, I had become alienated from 'left-wing' ideas as a young man through the cumulative effect of mind-numbing slogans, intolerance and lack of respect for the individual. However during my writing of this book I became more, rather than less sympathetic to the Left, that is to say the Left in its original form, when it was concerned with improving the lot of humanity as a whole, to giving individual men and women control over their own lives and fulfil their potential. This change of perspective strengthened my resolve against political correctness, because it undermines both freedom and social justice and is devouring the Left from within. I am, perhaps, especially tough on the feminist movement, because I believe that it has poisoned relationships between men and women, encouraging bitterness and competition, instead of the co-operation and compromise that greater parity of the sexes should have brought. Although I began the book feeling pessimistic, I finished with a renewed optimism that, in spite of the single-issue fanatics good sense might once again prevail. Those who wish to start on a positive note might therefore be advised to read the final chapter first and then work backwards. That chapter also takes account of the 'events' of September 11th, which have shaken the West's self-confidence because that confidence was superficial, as flimsy as the structures of the Twin Towers proved so regrettably to be.

I hope that this book will, over time, inspire some on the Left to abandon the narrow identity politics of race and gender. They might reflect that the political obsession with fulfilling pressure group demands resembles the corporate obsession with 'marketing niches'. The dissolving of traditional loyalties, be they patriotic, communitarian or familial, becomes a cultural counterpart to the agenda of transnational corporations, which regard such loyalties as quaint at best, but also potential sources of subversion. In that sense, political correctness and globalisation are not opposed to each other, as so many believe, but represent two sides of the same coin.

The cultural revolution promoted under the banner of political correctness aims to remove the sense of continuity and settled values that are our best recourse against irrational dogmas and arbitrary, convulsive changes over which we have little control. Conservatives have of late largely jettisoned any attempt to conserve anything, embracing a political correctness of the Right that worships the market above all. Indeed, just as there are signs that identity politics might be going out of fashion on the Left, conservatives are starting to embrace it. More thoughtful people from across the political spectrum are, nonetheless, beginning to see the need to reinvent civil society, to emphasise our shared concerns as citizens and human beings, rather than pandering to divisive pressure groups or corporate greed. This approach demands a balance between tradition and modernity. It is, as an excellent letter written recently to *The New Statesman* suggests, a true conservatism but a conservatism of the Left;

> I have felt for a long time that most of us on the left are not revolutionaries at heart, but really conservatives. We are conservatives in the sense of wanting to conserve the best in society: basic human dignity, the traditional sense of solidarity and the co-operative spirit.
>
> Our opposition to capitalism is based precisely on the fact that it destroys our basic humanity. … [I]t is capitalism that has been revolutionary in the sense of turning life upside down and smashing traditional values.
>
> The mass of the people will never be won to the banner of revolution because, in most people's minds, it represents chaos, uncertainty and a voyage into the unknown. Most of us want change for the better, but also want to hold on to those values, traditions and culture we are familiar with and like. If socialists emphasise their positive conservatism, rather than their revolutionary fervour and the joys of class

struggle, we might be able to persuade more ordinary people to join the movement for socialism. Long live revolutionary conservatism![1]

If we are to restore the political and economic processes of our time to anything like a human scale, we need to reclaim a common culture. That means abandoning the false gods and goddesses of political correctness, with all the prejudice and fear that their worship engenders.

Aidan Rankin
Settle, Yorkshire
June 2002

Acknowledgements

This book has been made possible by the support and friendship of John Coleman, as publisher, editor and mentor. Throughout my work on *The Politics of the Forked Tongue*, I have been stimulated and inspired by his shrewd comments and moderated by his wise counsel. The rallying support of Sir Richard Body has kept me enthused throughout. Helen Carroll proofread the manuscript and made me think about it a lot as well.

I am also most grateful to Diana Schumacher for her insightful remarks on my final chapter and her critical, stimulating commentary on the issues I address in the book. Lloyd Allen, as typesetter, has been an invaluable source of advice and help and Harry Tucker's marvellous illustration captures the essence of 'authoritarian liberalism' far better than any words.

Finally, I would like to thank those whose ideas and works I criticise, sometimes trenchantly, in these pages. I owe them much, because in criticising them, I question my own ideas, too, a process that will continue well beyond this book.

1. From Individual to Group: The Politics of Pressure

The scene with which I have chosen to begin this book is a dinner party in North London. This is a fitting, some might say too fitting, place to start a discussion of 'political correctness' in the British context, for North London is regarded by many as the heartland of 'liberal elitism'. Yet I cannot resist beginning there, for what occurred captures the essence of a new liberal mentality, or rather a new mentality that describes itself as liberal, but which has now become a threat to our liberty.

My host that night, who is both patient and apolitical, knew little of the dangers that lay ahead, when he combined me with his other guest, an American academic in late middle age, equipped with the armature of centre-left prejudices that have become commonplace on arts faculties. He was a homosexual who had once been married and had grown up children; I refer to his sexual orientation only because it is in some ways relevant to the discussion. The academic, who I shall call Jeff, lambasted me for belonging to one of the London men's clubs. Such establishments, he believed, were immoral because they discriminated against women. Furthermore, they should be made illegal, as they are in many cities throughout the Land of the Free and, he alleged, 'in Scandinavia'[1]. Men's clubs and women's clubs too (for the fellow was nothing if not consistent) deserved to be proscribed by 'the state' because the principle of 'equality' was more important than free association, more important, in some circumstances, than freedom itself. Discrimination is not a private matter but a public issue in which 'the state has a role'. Discrimination is not a 'right'. Gentlemen's clubs should be forced to admit women as members in the interests of 'universal human rights', which can 'never' be compromised and are more important than individual preferences. Besides, Jeff told me, clubs like mine are 'outmoded' and for this alone they 'should be abolished'.

I responded by declaring, somewhat tetchily no doubt and frivolously in new liberal eyes, that gentlemen's clubs emphatically do discriminate on grounds of sex. This, in itself, is no more reprehensible than philatelic clubs discriminating in favour of stamp collectors, hiking clubs discriminating against the sedentary, or Crufts giving prizes to dogs rather than cats, however beautiful and intelligent the latter might be. Indeed it would be strange for a gentlemen's club *not* to discriminate on sex grounds, since its purpose is to provide a friendly association for men. In this, there is no intention to hurt women, any more than philatelists wish to hurt coin collectors or the organisers of Crufts to offend the breeders of cats. A men's club is a men's club, after all, just as a dog show is a dog show. They serve distinct purposes. There are ladies' clubs and there are a wide variety of 'mixed' clubs, for both men and women. There are clubs for the religious and the atheistic, clubs for homosexuals only and clubs aimed specifically at the young. Only I choose to belong to a men's club, because I find it congenial. All the other clubs or societies I belong to, whether cultural, political or outdoor, are mixed, and these I value at least as highly. My choice to belong to a men's club does no harm to others, nor does it limit 'opportunity' for women, for it is not a professional association, like the Kennel Club or the Law Society. Nor does the existence of such clubs do any conceivable harm to others. Indeed, a society that men, young and old, enjoy is good for the wider society, for it helps to restrain our male energy and keeps us peaceful, placid and, for the most part, sober. Besides, I pointed out to Jeff, I was a much younger man than he and I do not consider men's clubs to be outdated or archaic. Even if they were so, that would not, of itself, be a cause for abolition.

Jeff then raised the emotional temperature by bringing in 'race'. This is a favourite tactic of new liberals, when they are on the defensive. Any form of 'discrimination' or any attempt to draw distinctions between people, except for the purposes of 'positive action' or group rights, is said to be the moral equivalent of racial prejudice and all the evils that spring from it. In this spirit, Jeff claimed that men's clubs that refused membership to women were 'as bad' as whites-only clubs in the dark days of segregation, that there was 'no difference at all' between 'racism' and 'sexism'. He suggested that, surely, my female friends would 'feel excluded' and that 'surely I wouldn't want that'. I agreed with him that women had, like black people in the West, well-founded historic grievances. It is right that these should be addressed, as should the more recent grievances of men and boys, who find themselves disadvantaged increasingly in educational provision and employment. There was, and remains, discrimination on grounds of race, sex and much else besides. It assumes ugly and often similar forms. These similarities, however, should not be taken to mean that they are precisely the same, or that they can always be tackled in identical ways. The principle of fair treatment for men and women, which is one of the hallmarks of civilisation, should not be reduced to making them wholly alike. The differences between the sexes are the stuff of biology at one level, poetry at another and constant debate amongst psychologists, teachers, academic feminists of varying hues and the opponents of feminism (male and female), whose arguments are equally varied. The nature of such differences might only be vaguely defined, but they exist, and all societies have found ways to recognise them. The Plains Indians, original inhabitants of Jeff's homeland, have Men's Societies and Women's Societies, between which social and ritual responsibilities are shared.[2] The Societies and their members complement each other, in communities that accord high status to women without downgrading masculinity in any respect. All-male and all-female groups are not, therefore, automatically comparable to racially segregated communities. They fulfil a natural function, create a healthy balance between the sexes and the opportunity for men and women to withdraw, temporarily, from each other's company when they so wish.

    This was followed by the angry assertion from Jeff that all-male societies were 'institutionally homophobic', that men who joined them were boys together, united in prejudice against homosexuals. This, to me, was a particularly bizarre accusation. I told Jeff that although the overwhelming majority of our members were heterosexuals, often with wives and children, homosexual men were equally welcome to join, whether they were openly homosexual or not. In the atmosphere of the club, heterosexual and homosexual men are friendly and courteous towards each other. Moreover, in the context of a single-sex club, there is no tension, nor any sense of grievance, between them, for sexual orientation is simply not an issue.

Furthermore, I speculated that were there moves to open the club to female membership, it would be the homosexual members who would object more strongly than, say, the crusty ex-military men with families scattered across the world. And they would be right to object, for they would lose the freedom to socialise on equal footing with their heterosexual peers. I appealed to Jeff's sympathy for his homosexual comrades, but he was unyielding. Homosexuals had no more right to discriminate than anyone else. As 'victims' of discrimination themselves, they had a 'duty' to be 'sensitive'. Furthermore, 'gays and lesbians' were working together for 'equal rights' in employment, partnership laws equivalent to marriage, 'parenting rights' and 'full equality' with 'straight people'. If the gay rights groups got their way, the homosexual men in my club would lose the freedom to associate with men only, but they would 'gain' many glorious new 'rights' in return. This, Jeff lectured me, would solve all their 'problems' and compensate for their loss of an all-male group. Being liberated from 'homophobic oppression', they would lose the desire to belong to all-male clubs in any case, much as, presumably, the Soviet Union's 'liberated' workers were supposed to lose their belief in God. As for those evil heterosexual men who wanted an all-male group, their opinions counted for nothing. They 'must learn' that they have 'no right to discriminate against anybody'.

It was clear by this time that we had reached an impasse, and that our disagreement reached far beyond the desirability of men's clubs. That question was, in some ways, a ruse by which more profound differences of philosophy could be further explored. Both of us regarded ourselves as liberals, in that the society we believed in would be as free, and as just to its citizens, as was practically possible. But much as George Bernard Shaw once remarked that the Americans and the British were divided by a common language, so Jeff and I were divided by our common liberalism. I, the younger man, was an old liberal. He, the older man, was a new liberal, or rather his was to my mind a mutation of liberalism, with some distinctly authoritarian overtones. It was clear that Jeff and I differed primarily on the role of the state in the individual's life, the balance between 'freedom' and 'equality' and the nature of both these concepts. Rather than merely protect freedom, Jeff believed, the state defined and 'enforced' it. Like Jean-Jacques Rousseau, he felt that man, both individually and in the group, may be 'forced to be free' by collective action, that the individual (in

Rousseau's own words) 'becomes an intelligent being and a man' when he submits to the General Will. That freedom bears little relationship to personal choice, but to a collectivist idea of 'liberation' as a form of group-think. Those who reject it are not truly free. Either they are oppressing themselves, because of past conditioning, or they are suffering from 'false consciousness'. In other words, they do not know that they are oppressed and need to be told that they are by those with superior knowledge. Or rather, they need to be 'liberated' by the state – or self-appointed activists - whether they wish for that liberation or not.

Accordingly, men's clubs are inherently oppressive. Changing their membership rules was an issue of human rights, but the rights of the men in the club did not count because they had the 'wrong' interpretation of rights. Many members of the club were judged (without evidence) to be active oppressors – closet misogynists or more overt 'homophobes'. Others – the homosexual members in particular – were guilty of oppressing themselves. Far from being further oppressed by legislation, these men 'would clearly benefit' from changes to the law.[3] These changes would 'enable' such men to become 'politically mature' and to realise that their 'true interests' lay in uniting with lesbians, feminists and 'minority groups' in a struggle to 'end all discrimination'. I then asked Jeff what he thought about homosexuals who did not want any of the 'rights' being demanded by their self-appointed spokesmen, who disliked the idea of 'uniting' with lesbians and merely wished to be left alone – something that had been achieved in Britain more than thirty years ago but was yet to be achieved in all American states.[4] Jeff was predictably opposed to American sodomy laws. These, he claimed (erroneously) existed solely in 'redneck' states, surely a culturally biased assumption in itself. 'Gay men' had a responsibility to work with lesbians because they shared a 'common oppression' and confronted a common 'enemy': heterosexuals, or more specifically heterosexual men. 'Straight' men, he told me, 'also oppress women' and so the gay and feminist causes were the same. Homosexual men who 'did not see this' were leading 'restricted lives' and 'colluding with prejudice'. I asked about unprejudiced heterosexual men. 'That's no problem,' Jeff replied. 'They see things from our point of view and are prepared to work with us'. All those who did not work with 'us' were 'prejudiced' by definition. As to their intended fates, I did not inquire.

The contradictions in these arguments should be patently obvious. It is surely extraordinary, after all, to believe that other people can be set free from restricted lives by having their lives still further restricted by the state. The catalogue of name-calling and 'common enemies' typifies residual left-wing thought: revolutionary socialism without the economics, of which the affluent protesters of the 1960s generation thought little. Also derived from the left is the essentially elitist notion that the majority are unknowingly 'oppressed' or 'oppressing themselves', often through ignorance but sometimes wilfully, through backward, outdated beliefs and customs. It was the task of revolutionaries to enable 'the masses' to see clearly their oppression and turn against their oppressors. In the post-1789 era, those 'masses' have generally been the urban poor, the rural peasantry, the industrial working class and 'Third World' peoples. They are 'revolutionary classes', the agents of change whether they wish it or know it. But in the modern epoch, the perennial problem for revolutionaries and radicals of all shades has been communicating with members of 'their' class (or race) so that they will awake from intellectual slumber – and in the process give power to a revolutionary elite. As one historian of revolutionary thought and praxis puts it:

> Thoughtful revolutionaries in the 1880s began to realise that there must be some better way [than spontaneous protest] of overcoming the failure of communication between the revolutionaries themselves, who came from a relatively cultured background, and the working class who were not only suspicious of intellectuals but had little stomach for revolution and could not in any case be expected to understand the issues involved or to judge the action required. It was this realisation which led one of the Russian revolutionaries, Tkachev, to evolve the theory of the 'revolutionary vanguard', which later formed the basis of Lenin's philosophy.

> Revolutions, Tkachev said, could not be successfully conducted unless they were led by a highly trained, and dedicated elite (the cadres). Tkachev also described what has subsequently become known as a 'revolutionary situation'. The revolutionary elite must not attempt to seize power until there is 'a general sense of impunity' – in other words, when the people as a whole begin to believe that the government lacks either the will or the power to enforce its laws.

> Tkachev and his fellow nineteenth century revolutionaries, however, did not give enough thought to the fact that the mass of the people

must still be organised and led if power was to be seized and held. It was Lenin, with his genius for organisation and propaganda and his sensitive nose for public feeling, who put Tkachev's theories into action.[5]

The idea of the revolutionary vanguard is radically anti-democratic and illiberal. It is based on 'talking down to' and manipulating 'the masses', taking advantage of their immediate grievances but twisting them towards a larger, more abstract goal. It means ignoring the needs and wishes of the 'oppressed' class, both as a group and as individuals, if these conflict with the overriding aim of revolutionary change. It also means thwarting or sabotaging reforms, because these make revolution less likely. Often, it means goading the 'class enemy' into repressive actions, or behaving in ways that increase economic, social or cultural divisions.[6] The underlying illiberal character of revolutionary vanguard theory helps to explain why revolutions conducted on this basis have invariably produced dictatorships. For if anything at all is historically inevitable, it is that this form of revolutionary change will be authoritarian, coercive and enacted without any attempt to take account of, let alone respect, alternative views of the world or individual experience that conflicts with its dogma. Revolutionary vanguard theory is based on that very lack of respect, on the assumption by small groups of activists that those they seek to emancipate are either stupid, or 'mystified' or both, that they quite literally 'don't know what's good for them'. And so the vanguard takes it upon itself to separate sheep from goats, to classify 'oppressor' and 'oppressed' and treat them accordingly. Both the oppressor classes and the oppressed are identified exclusively as members of groups, with their individual desires, opinions and peculiarities wholly subordinated to group identity. This means that members of the oppressed classes can be dealt with as harshly as the oppressors if they refuse to welcome their liberators.

The disdain for ordinary people – and ordinary human reality – evinced by left-wing activists has been remarked upon frequently enough and it has done much to undermine the left on occasions when it might have been a force for good. Revolutionaries carry that disdain a stage further into contempt for human life. This results in a willingness to sacrifice millions of lives, and ruin millions more, to achieve the 'ultimate goal' of equality. Stalin, whose policy of agricultural collectivisation killed millions, is said to have observed: 'one death is a tragedy, one million deaths are a statistic'. Beatrice Webb, whose Fabian brand of state socialism was non-violent, but authoritarian and deterministic notwithstanding, found in the Bolshevik Revolution hope for mankind's progress. Of the political murders that took place in the aftermath of 1917, she observed that in order to make an omelette, you have to break some eggs. Lenin, whose background was irretrievably bourgeois, believed that he possessed special insights into what workers really needed, as opposed to what they thought they wanted. 'The workers, left to themselves, are capable only of trade union consciousness,' he proclaimed in what must be one of the most patronising political pronouncements of modern times. This limited consciousness on the part of the workers was exactly why they should not be 'left to themselves'. Instead they should be saved from themselves, or more importantly, the ideal of revolution must be saved from their stupidity and short sightedness. The antipathy to 'trade union consciousness' is an antipathy to incremental political and economical reforms of the kind that work with the grain of society and human nature, rather than seeking to change the character of both. It is hostility to the attempt, by liberals and 'reformist' social democrats, to treat individuals and communities fairly, to address injustices on a case-by-case basis, rather than pursue rigid 'equality for all'.

Contempt for 'the masses' has pervaded left-wing movements. Under democratic conditions, this narrow form of elitism limited their popularity, overshadowed their reasoned critiques of unrestrained capitalism and discouraged their more humane leaders or activists.[7] The idea of a revolutionary vanguard that defines the interests of 'the people' for them has been used to rationalise the seizure of power and the extinction of individual freedom by a plethora of regimes in Eastern Europe, East Asia and Africa since 1917, most of which fell because they were as inefficient and wasteful as they were oppressive. The idea of a revolutionary vanguard is not, by any means, unique to Marxist thought. Indeed it at once predates and outlives orthodox Communism as a significant political force.[8] However it has arguably been more destructive to Marxist politics than any of the original flaws in Marxist theory. Beyond Marxism, the idea of the vanguard has cast a cloud over the entire left, so that there is a tendency on the part even of moderate socialists – and liberal reformers – to believe that they are 'freeing' others from 'false consciousness' and that this can justify repressive acts.

How did we move from a dinner party discussion about the rights and wrongs of men's clubs to a consideration of revolutionary theory and its consequences? What, if anything, connects these two apparently distinctive issues, one small and specific, the other abstract and large? For the answer we must come back to the new liberal idea that 'the personal is political'. Applied practically, this means that everything in human society is connected to everything else, that all divisions between human activities are artificial, especially the division between the public and private realm. There is a sense in which genuine liberals and cultural conservatives[9] also believe this. But theirs is a holistic view of politics, which tolerates, indeed welcomes, divergence and difference, seeing society as akin to a living organism, an ecosystem or a work of traditional craftsmanship instead of an idealised design. Greens, at least those untouched by politically correct jargon, take this idea a stage further, seeing an intimate connection between biodiversity and cultural diversity, between preserving wilderness or forests and allowing indigenous peoples to maintain their social systems and their unique cultures. Far from holistic, the new liberal view is rigid and (to use Jeff's word) restrictive. It sees connections between human activities, but only in the interests of a general levelling or a quest to define common standards and impose them universally.

The failure of Soviet 'socialism' has not destroyed the far left, much of which had rejected the Soviet model decades before the Cold War ended. Nor has it dampened revolutionary enthusiasm for reshaping mankind. It has, however, obscured the radical left's larger aims. Whilst they still work towards 'socialism', 'workers' control' or 'common ownership' and believe that these are historically inevitable, left-wing activists devote far less effort than in the recent past to defining their long-term goals. Like more old-fashioned Marxists, they participate in and seek to control reformist campaigns, but unlike orthodox Communists they lack a coherent strategy for political change. The collapse of orthodox Communism has led, on the left as a whole, to the eclipse of economic philosophy and a fanatical preoccupation with social or cultural issues. This shift of emphasis has helped to obscure the division between traditional liberalism and the radical left. Liberals, who are also interested in social issues, now find it easier to unite with radicals who speak the language of civil liberties without referring excessively to economic change: the abolition of private property has yielded to vaguer ideas of social justice, blueprints for economic equality have given way to a fanatical cult of 'Equal Opportunities'.

Paradoxically, the liberal ideal of open-minded tolerance can lead many well-meaning, thoughtful men and women towards adopting intolerant positions. They take at face value the far left's[10] commitment to civil liberties and human rights and so are likely to accept far left interpretations of these ideals as valid, or even to place them beyond all questioning. Such interpretations are always collectivist in character, but they are expressed with a sense of certainty and a volubility that most traditional liberals are unable to match. Rather than be shouted down, as they were in the universities of the 1960s and 70s, they are often prepared to allow their ideals of individual freedom to wither away, under the pretext of modernisation and 'moving on'. Or, in the interests of a quiet life, they will permit the language of freedom to be used as a weapon against liberty. Furthermore, the far left and single-issue activists are adept at claiming to speak on behalf of oppressed or minority groups, at claiming to provide a voice for the voiceless. Self-declared representatives of these groups are routinely produced to give 'the black perspective', 'a woman's perspective' or 'the "lesbian and gay" view'. Liberals have found this tactic especially hard to resist, in part because of guilt arising from a misguided interpretation of recent history, in part because of a genuine desire to help those who are oppressed or hard-done-by, but mostly because of their sheer lack of knowledge or interest.

Just as they take at face value the revolutionary left's conversion to human rights, liberals are often ready to accept that militant, bigoted 'anti-racists' speak for all 'ethnic minorities', that 'gender' feminists speak for women and that gay activists (of any sex) articulate the views of homosexual men.[11] In modern politics, there is an in-built tendency to classify individuals conveniently as members of groups and assume in them a common response. There is also, in members of any majority population, however liberal, a tendency to lump together those who differ from them, of whose lives they have little experience, or whom they regard as 'other'.[12] Thus there is little psychological difference between a liberal man's acceptance that radical feminists speak for all women and a Protestant's assumption that all Catholics oppose all forms of birth control except for the rhythm method. There is the same failure to evaluate, the same lazy thinking (which is the undoing of liberalism) and, ultimately, the same set of prejudices. Single-issue activists claim, with forked tongues, to be opposed to prejudice or, in their preferred vocabulary, to be forever 'challenging stereotypes'. However they depend on these stereotypes, and the prejudices that inform them, to sway liberal opinion and implant the idea of group rights instead of individual freedom within civil society. In the interests of 'liberation', collective stereotypes are perpetuated. Those who oppose them are condemned as bigots if they are white, male or 'straight', as turncoats if they are black[13], female or 'gay'.

Once more with forked tongues, the advocates of group rights claim to increase the visibility of those previously excluded from public life. At the same time, they do their utmost to render invisible any members of 'their' groups who disagree with them. They achieve this through a judicious blend of emotional blackmail, threats and violent denunciations, as well as a more insidious trickle-down effect by which their propaganda influences mainstream liberals.[14] Those same liberals embrace authoritarian, collectivist solutions to the 'problems' presented by 'minority groups'. In this way, a spirit of authoritarian collectivism spreads well beyond the far left, so that liberals, along with democratic socialists and a growing number of conservatives, are ready to place the group before the individual and give professional activists the power to speak and act for those 'communities' – often fictitious in themselves – that they are claiming to represent.

The result of all this is a vanguard of bureaucrats, pressure groups and unrepresentative 'community leaders' drunk with power, who have a vested interest in perpetuating prejudice under the guise of opposing it. Invariably, their language is that of aggression and combat, replete with exhortations to fight racism, eliminate sexism and confront homophobia. These quasi-military metaphors belie one of the principal claims of single-issue activism, namely that its purpose is to reduce hatred, create greater social cohesion and extend opportunity. In reality, single-issue campaigns very quickly lapse into outpourings of hatred and blame. Group rights are reinforced by group wrongs, because the collective emancipation of oppressed groups requires the collective castigation of the oppressors. Thus, instead of taking the individual as the starting point and aiming at fairness to all, the various movements against discrimination delight in blaming 'men' for the oppression of women, 'straight society' for prejudice against homosexuals and 'whites' for racial prejudice. The irony of blaming a racial group collectively for racial prejudice is lost on anti-racist campaigners. Their campaigns, along with parallel activities on behalf of 'women' and 'gays', are organised as if they were intended to provoke a violent backlash, or at least smouldering rage, from members of those groups demonised as oppressors, whatever, as individuals, they might have done.

Far from stopping with white heterosexual men, the demonising process gleefully extends to the oppressed who refuse to play ball. Women who prefer family life to a career, 'closeted' homosexual men who refuse to 'come out'[15] and black people who show no interest in 'fighting racism' are just as much the objects of politically correct hate speech. The nexus of anti-discrimination campaigns and state sponsored social intervention creates a professional cadre of bureaucrats with a vested interest in creating new forms of prejudice and new roles for the state in combating them. Thus appointment on merit becomes 'institutionalised racism' (to the detriment of gifted 'non-whites' who have been solely appointed on merit).[16] Likewise, men and women choosing separate roles, careers and activities becomes 'sexual apartheid' or 'gender segregation', whilst the principle of non-discrimination gives way to 'positive action', which means discrimination in reverse. State sponsored anti-discrimination campaigns must justify their existence by proposing new laws, launching new bureaucratic initiatives and looking for new ways to regulate the lives of citizens. At a time when market forces dominate economic thinking, when public utilities are starved of funds and sold off, when manufacturing industry and farming are both allowed to go to the wall, the anti-discrimination industry proliferates unchecked, at public expense, growing ever more dictatorial and intrusive, both to those who oppose it and those it is claiming to help.

The left's retreat from economics has had two effects, both closely related to each other. First, it has led to an overwhelming focus on questions of identity, as defined by ethnic group or skin colour, by whether one is male and female, attracted to the opposite sex or one's own. The idea of class struggle, once so important to the Marxist analysis of society, is supplanted by a polarisation of races, a reverse racism in which 'white' Western culture is viewed as a legitimate target.[17] In the sexual sphere, the class system yields to a 'gender system' in which relationships between women and men become a battleground: the class struggle, between exploiting and exploited classes, is translated into a 'gender' struggle against masculinity and male dominance, the outcome of which is androgyny, the feminist counterpart to the classless society. The issue of race has, for nearly two centuries, loomed large in liberal and left wing circles, and rightly so, because of the oppression and injustice that have stemmed from racial prejudice, or the conquest of one race by another. However socialists, and to a lesser extent traditional liberals, have seen the emancipation of all races as part of a wider movement towards a more equitable social order, at home and on the international stage. In pursuing this aim, they seek to reduce racial conflict and promote shared values, without undermining distinctive cultures or compromising national identities. New liberals, by contrast, play upon and often encourage conflict between races, for they see it as part of the political struggle.

Liberals and the left have also championed the emancipation of women, so that they can, as individuals, contribute towards a more just society. In this sense, the emancipation of women is the emancipation of men as well, unlike radical feminism, which disparages masculinity (whilst at the same time mimicking its worst aspects) and seeks to degrade or discriminate against men. The obsession with race, and the racism-in-reverse to which it leads, is a new phenomenon, as is the relentless focus on sexual issues, acerbically dismissed by Ralph Nader, the American environmentalist, as 'gonadal politics'. Considerations of race, sex and sexuality now override economic concerns, so that it becomes quite possible for fanatical advocates of racial equality to be indifferent to poverty, white and black. Poverty and gross disparity of income thereby become acceptable as long as they cross whatever racial divides exist. Meanwhile, the emphasis of much feminist activity shifts from creating a more humane, or human-scale, society towards placing more women in the boardrooms of transnational corporations, so they too can exploit the poor – often the black poor – of both sexes. The gay rights movement prides itself on the advent of 'pink capitalism' that emphasises income and appearance over intelligence and character, portraying as liberation for men the regime of superficiality from which intelligent women have long since freed themselves. The compatibility of single-issue rights campaigns with consumerism and gross social injustice has ensured their spread beyond left-wing circles, often as a convenient diversion or as a marketing opportunity for big business. Single-issue politics has become the dominant discourse on the left at the behest of the pampered children of the 1960s, for whom political protest was often not much more than a collective tantrum. Their values are far removed from those of the workers and the intellectuals who have formed the backbone of genuine left wing movements. Being products of affluence, the sixties generation were ultimately unlikely to favour any broader vision of humanity that might challenge materialistic values. The personal might now be political, but both political and personal issues are placed conveniently before the more difficult economic questions.

The second, closely associated, effect of the left's retreat from economics has been a more general shift from the 'macro' to the 'micro', from broader concerns with the economy and society towards far more trivial issues involving the way people lead their lives. This means that a great deal of left-wing activity is focused on extremely petty concerns, such as the membership policies of private clubs, for in the absence of a coherent economic philosophy these loom increasingly large. The previous focus on larger questions of economic and social organisation was often detrimental to the Left, because it meant that theory was placed before practice, abstract ideals before awkward human truths. At its worst, this concentration on theory led to totalitarianism, whether of the Soviet model, the Maoist version in China or the Trotskyist variant of Marxism-Leninism that has never really been tested in power.[18]

In the more democratic context, excessive emphasis on abstract theory can easily result in social policies that lack imaginative sympathy for those individuals and communities they are intended to 'help'. The most notorious example is, perhaps, the destruction of urban working-class terraces and their replacement by soulless housing estates and high-rise flats. That decision, in the confident aftermath of World War II, was made without consulting the affected communities, on the assumption that formally trained experts invariably knew best.[19] A similar belief in expertise, coupled with a missionary desire to improve or 'civilise', informed Canadian governments[20] in the same era, when they built villages for native peoples and imposed policies of forced settlement. In both cases, personal and cultural pride were lost, along with traditions of voluntary co-operation and self-help that held communities together. In both cases, misguided expertise contributed to a cycle of family breakdown, addiction and crime, along with aesthetic and emotional deprivation. The failure of centralised planning, both in democratic and totalitarian contexts, has led to a crisis of confidence on the left, a questioning of basic assumptions about economics and a move away from more obvious or grandiloquent forms of social engineering.

From this crisis of ideology on the left, one might conclude that the principle of refashioning human society has been abandoned, in favour of pragmatic liberalism and piecemeal reform. Much of the economic rhetoric of New Labour in Britain or the New Democrats in the United States would indicate this trend[21]. In practice, however, much of the centre left appears to have embraced the ideology of market forces with a fervour that a conservative would tend to consider bad form. Lenin once described communism as socialism plus electrification. The centre left's 'Third Way' might be considered in similar terms, as market forces plus political correctness. In abandoning socialist economics, or consigning them to a distant, dimly envisioned future, the left as a whole has jettisoned some disastrous dogmas. At the same time, the left has lost what might justly be described as a spiritual dimension, a generosity and breadth of vision that distinguished it from the right, and which has often resulted in humane legislation. Yet the retreat from economics and the abandonment of large-scale social projects has not meant that the left has relinquished its commitment to social engineering. On the contrary, the efforts of left-wing campaigners in this direction are ever more zealous. They also affect the individual in a more immediate sense, because they encroach directly upon the way he chooses to lead his life.

The new left-wing zeal is widely referred to as political correctness, originally an ironic sobriquet but now part of everyday discourse. An important aspect of 'PC' is its lack of any reasonable sense of proportion, as if its proponents were incapable of distinguishing between the significant and the trivial, or for doctrinaire reasons refuse to do so. There is also a sense in which a focus on narrow and petty issues of language and behaviour is a form of compensation for the absence of any credible economic and social theory, about which the post-Cold War left is very defensive. The fall of Communism in Europe – which despite its obvious flaws held out the possibility of another way of organising society – has been the source of much frustration on the left, compounded by the seemingly irresistible rise of global capitalism. The failure of socialists, and those left-liberals who incline towards socialism, to evaluate and frame a response to these events, has created a climate of bitterness and recrimination. Leftwingers who feel that they have lost control of the economic and social debate now address minor points of principle with a determination once reserved for 'the big questions'. Several previous generations of the left debated revolution versus reform, the 'parliamentary road to socialism' versus strikes and sabotage, or whether socialist industries should be controlled by the state or self-managed by the workers. Their post-modern successors, by contrast, fret over the existence of men's clubs or attempt to stop boys in the playground from firing toy guns at each other. They affect outrage at those who tell jokes about foreigners in the pub, or who stick to the male pronoun instead of adopting priggishly inelegant 'inclusive language'.

Such illiberal and vindictive obsessions seem to signify powerlessness, or even a sense of vulnerability. There is a sense in which politically correct campaigners resemble litigious neighbours in a suburban street, or the needling, puritanical 'wowsers' of popular Australian culture. They are, nonetheless, a potent social force instead of a mere local irritant. This is because they are well organised and often politically astute. Like the radical left of old, such campaigners are adept at exploiting the weaknesses of opponents and allies alike. Chief amongst these, usually, are lack of political analysis and a lack of certainty, although the latter should not be seen as a weakness at all, and would not be in a less extreme political climate. Political moderates, be they small-c conservative or liberal-left by inclination, are prepared to envisage other possibilities. These include the possibility that they might be wrong, or that their opponent has justice on his side.[22] The flexibility and tolerance of political liberalism, which should be its greatest strength, can easily become a weakness when faced with extremist demands. We have observed already that the liberal often overlooks the unrepresentative nature of single-issue movements, taking at face value their claims to 'speak for' their chosen group. Similarly, because his motives are essentially benign, he is likely to accept that extremist campaigns are really about 'rights' and 'freedoms' for oppressed sections of society, rather than power and careers for activists. Extremists also know that beyond a certain point the liberal does not care about politics, because he has other interests and priorities. This sense of ultimate indifference means that the liberal will often fail to recognise extremism when he sees it, or if he does suspect extremist motives, he fails to be perturbed by them in any significant way. Such indifference extends to the 'oppressed groups' for whom activists claim to speak. The liberal is therefore unlikely to find out what members of these groups *really* think. He is therefore inclined, for convenience and expediency, to sign away the rights of ethnic minorities to self-proclaimed community leaders, or those of homosexuals to 'lesbian and gay' campaigners who are unrepresentative to the point of absurdity. Such lack of concern can look, at times, like cold-hearted cynicism. Sometimes it is, but more often it is based on benign equanimity, combined with a singular lack of imagination.

These limits to the liberal imagination become particularly apparent when politically correct demands are raised. Because they arise over seemingly minor issues, it is tempting for liberals to believe that they do not 'really matter' to the majority of the population. If, the argument runs, politically correct demands pose no significant threat to liberty for most, and might enhance the rights of some, then why not give into them for the greater good? The sheer volubility and insistence of politically correct campaigners, and their relentlessness, suggests that failure to concede will lead to interminable battles. For most liberals, such battles seem pointless and trivial. They have forgotten that the price of freedom is eternal vigilance, although they recite this phrase as if it were a mantra. In their response to political correctness, liberals are deceived by the apparent triviality of the demands and by the activists' appeals to rights, freedom and dignity, the traditional liberal rallying cries. They are handicapped too by another of political liberalism's weaknesses, the failure to make connections. As pragmatists, who believe in assessing each specific issue on its merits, they do not readily grasp that individual acts of censorship on grounds of alleged 'racism', 'sexism' or, more recently, 'incitement to religious hatred', can be part of a far wider assault on freedom of speech. Likewise, the wish to outlaw single-sex clubs (voiced by many new liberals besides Jeff) is part of a larger attack on freedom of association, which is a founding principle of the modern liberal state, and which distinguishes a free society from an authoritarian or totalitarian regime.

Liberals, therefore, tend to acquiesce in the erosion of personal freedom, in misguided educational experiments, in 'anti-racist' campaigns that are themselves racially – and socially – biased. They wish to be seen to support 'equality' and 'progress' and fear above all the charges of prejudice or 'elitism'.[23] Anxious neither to offend nor upset, they prove unwilling to 'stick their necks out' in the face of determined campaigns. The result is a series of surrenders of liberal principles that begins to amount to a wholesale surrender. So pallid has liberal resistance been to politically correct assaults on freedom that the entire meaning of liberalism has been compromised. Many liberals, who still genuinely believe in freedom, have accepted so much of the collectivist agenda of group rights and so many restrictions on personal freedom, that they have become unwitting (and usually unwilling) authoritarians. Politically correct activists have an advantage over liberals, whom they deride as naïve in much the same way as Lenin spoke of humanitarian sympathisers as 'useful idiots'. For although they have no economic philosophy and only a confused vision of what a new society would be like, they have retained the revolutionary left's contempt for 'bourgeois' institutions and 'bourgeois' freedoms. For the term bourgeois they substitute phrases such as 'institutionally racist', 'sexist' or 'homophobic', but the hostility remains at least as strong.

2. The One-Size-Fits-All-Society

Unlike old liberals, politically correct campaigners recognise that minor issues of freedom of association amount to much more than trivial issues of convenience or taste. Together, they define the difference between a free society, with the individual as its starting point and a collectivist society where the group matters more than the individual and group identities are assigned by the state.[1] Politically correct campaigns, be they against toy guns, gentlemen's (and working men's) clubs, or 'racist' comedians can be seen as a series of pincer movements against individual freedom, fairness and tolerance. Political correctness itself is far from being, as it might often appear, a series of disconnected parts, or fragments of a dismembered radical left of sixties vintage. Although based on a series of single issues, it possesses a unified, uncompromising ideology, with an effective strategy to back it up, but no ultimate goal except for an ill-considered 'equality'. When this is defined at all, it is in terms of equality between groups, with no reference made to individual needs and tastes, or whether individuals should receive fair treatment. Equality is comprised of rights, presented by pressure groups as demands, implemented by the state[2] through court rulings, charters and edicts, along with intrusive pieces of legislation. It is enforced by vigilant activists in collusion with state and corporate bureaucrats, who work outside any recognisable democratic process.

Significantly, politically correct 'equality' is expressed in social and cultural, rather than economic terms. Those who work for a politically correct society use their strident, emotional hatred of privilege to justify attempts to impose uniformity, a 'level playing field' which suppresses difference, in which everyone has 'the same chance' – to succeed or (more usually) to fail. This spirit of levelling informed the 'comprehensivisation' of many British schools through the 1970s; in American public schools, too, the push towards egalitarianism can be fanatical and extreme. Yet such 'equality of opportunity' is deemed compatible with gross disparities of income, or more than that, it provides a useful justification for imbalances of wealth. In the Looking-Glass world of political correctness, liberals become authoritarian collectivists without knowing it, whilst the principle of equality is used to advance the principle of inequality. This forked-tongued position, inequality in the name of equality, affects politically correct campaigns at every level. From the traditional left, they inherit the idea of attacking tradition and punishing privilege. But unlike socialists of the old school, they accept, at times with relish, inequalities conferred by market forces. In the name of equality, too, some groups are favoured at the expense of others: women at the expense of men, for instance, or selected 'minorities' over the 'ethnic majority'.[3] Racial prejudice is held up as a greater social ill than poverty, although it is poverty that crosses racial lines and at the same time fuels racial tensions.

In political correctness, the punitive aspect of the left survives, without any compensating ideals of generosity or compassion. The idea of the revolutionary vanguard persists in the single issue pressure groups of identity politics that take up cudgels against racism, patriarchy or 'straight society', but in so doing make assumptions about black people, women and homosexuals that are as stereotypical as their opponents' prejudices.[4] Pressure groups assume almost Gnostic insights into those sections of society they purport to represent. They assume the ability to interpret their needs, wishes and political insights for them, without even the pretence of consultation. Those who oppose pressure group politics and do not belong to 'oppressed groups' are dismissed as bigots, as reactionaries and as sub-human enemies to be banished from political life. Those who are classified as oppressed, but who regard the activities of pressure groups as patronising and truly oppressive, are first cajoled with sentimental pleas and then denounced with a particular venom reserved for those labelled as traitors. A case in point is the practice, adopted by some gay rights organisations, of 'outing' or publicly exposing as homosexual political opponents who have not declared their sexual orientation. They justify this form of oppression on quasi-moral grounds as exposing hypocrisy, adding with Puritan piety that the individuals in question brought it upon themselves. The use of outing as a campaigning tool shows that the purpose of such activist groups is control rather than emancipation, that they wish to induce conformity amongst 'their' constituents rather than serve any representative function. Outing also revives the outdated stereotype of the homosexual as blackmailer or victim of blackmail, for it is crude intimidation given a politically correct gloss. Its message – if you don't vote 'our' way we shall expose you – has been the prerogative of the blackmailer throughout the ages.[5]

Of equal significance, during our dinner party discussion, was the special ire that Jeff expressed for the homosexuals who join all-male clubs. He dismissed the heterosexual majority as bigoted beyond redemption. The homosexuals, by contrast, were 'confused' men in need of 'consciousness-raising'. This notion has some uncomfortable totalitarian connotations, calling to mind the re-education or thought reform programmes adopted by some Marxist regimes.[6] It is also reminiscent of a 'they don't know what's good for them' attitude adopted by more conventional busybodies, which presages inept and destructive attempts at reform. Traditional liberalism has encompassed many 'do-gooders' who are ridiculed for their efforts, sometimes unjustly but often because in their enthusiasm to improve other people's lives, they fail to listen to others or reflect on the consequences of their actions. There is a missionary impulse in liberal thought that sometimes finds literal expression in missionary activities. More often, in recent times especially, it takes a secular form. 'Development' charities and non-governmental organisations act as magnets for liberal missionaries who wish to serve abroad. Closer to home, they busy themselves with campaigns for new laws, new rights and the 'modernisation' of institutions, in the belief that structural change will create more rational and hence more virtuous human beings.

Rationalisation, in practice, usually means attempts at standardisation. This is based on the idea that if everybody is treated the same or roughly the same, then a fairer society will result. The problem with this attractive notion is that it works only when it is applied with moderation and good sense. The notion of equality before the law, for example, is an essential guarantor of liberty. Universal provision of health care and access to education in the broadest sense, not just academic schooling, are also crucial ingredients of an equitable society. Such benign principles quickly become perverted when there is a failure to allow for individual, cultural or regional differences, or when successful practices are discounted in favour of untried theories. Then, equality is placed before freedom (to the detriment of both principles) and obsessive rationalism becomes an irrational end in itself. Some recent examples, as noted above, include over-zealous campaigns against educational diversity or attempts to deny intrinsic differences between male and female behaviour and needs. They extend to the replacement of traditional working class communities by soulless housing estates and high-rise towers, the introduction of laws that encourage family breakdown rather than long-term commitment, or the creation of anti-discrimination industries that in practice perpetuate social division.

The political vocabulary of liberalism is ill equipped to express a sense of failure. When rationalising liberals see that their prescriptions have not worked, they rarely admit to failure or return to the drawing board. On the contrary, they will claim that their reforms have not gone far enough, that there should be more, rather than less, educational uniformity, more 'anti-discrimination' laws and, as an extension, 'positive discrimination' – inequality to achieve equality. Accompanying the optimism of liberal thought has always been a degree of arrogance. Liberals are quick to be impatient when those they wish to help refuse to co-operate with them. They are surprised and angered when people react unpredictably, or in ways wholly different from the ways that the reformers had in mind. This anger and impatience may lead the liberal to condone the use of force, or be attracted to collectivist programmes, which have coercion at their centre.

In this way, the activist mentality of the new liberalism gives to the old missionary impulse an extreme edge. Onto the more traditional do-goodery is grafted a revolutionary imperative that takes even less account of individual needs than missionary liberalism and has fewer scruples about using force. In its crude form, revolutionary Marxism has demonised conservative working men as 'class collaborators'. Politically correct campaigners have adopted this tactic and applied it to questions of racial and sexual politics. In identity politics, the pressure group becomes the equivalent of a revolutionary vanguard. Its aim is not to represent the 'oppressed' identities, but to write policy for them and, more than that, to determine how they should think and feel. This was the underlying cause of Jeff's anger that homosexuals, as well as 'sexist' heterosexual men, should enjoy all-male clubs and his dismay that homosexuals could themselves be 'sexist' (hardly an earth-shattering revelation for anyone other than a left-leaning academic). To his way of thinking, such men are guilty of something more heinous than 'discrimination', sinful though this is. Their main fault is refusal to behave in the way that gay activists expect of them, namely ally themselves with lesbians and feminists against the 'straight' male enemy.

For the pressure groups and their allies, it is either 'our way or no way' to liberation. The activist mentality refuses to accept that some individuals make different choices from those favoured by pressure groups. Those who make such choices are 'wrong' and so must be brought into line and forced to conform. The revolutionary element in the new liberalism aims to cajole and punish, the moralistic element to plead and persuade. As a result, politically correct campaigns are pervaded by authoritarianism and sentimentality. They lack the human understanding and the intellectual flexibility to cope with those who dissent from the new 'party lines' and seek to carve out a different path for themselves.[7]

The moralistic element in political correctness distinguishes it ideologically from Marxism, which aims at objective or scientific analysis. It shares orthodox Marxism's main blind spot – the failure to take account of individual variations – and unites it with liberalism's quest for ethical purity. Politically correct campaigns combine a Pharisaic obsession with laws and structures, and a hyper-rationalist attitude to human nature[8], with an appeal to emotion and a romantic tendency to place feeling before reason. This leads to a wide range of inconsistencies, although, as hyper-rationalism is itself quite unreasonable, there is a greater underlying unity than at first might appear. One of the main points of unity is the use of force, whether it is to reshape human nature, at the more abstract level, or more prosaically to curb the behaviour of recalcitrant individuals and 'enemy' groups.

Politically correct campaigners draw no distinction between the abstract and the prosaic, except insofar as they emphasise the latter because they lack a clear vision of what Utopia would be like. In this emphasis on petty restrictions, they resemble the Puritans, whose Utopia was otherworldly and who combined an austere rationalism with an appeal to the emotions and a rigid egalitarian consciousness. Political correctness, and identity-based movements generally, originate in the United States and exert a more powerful influence over

American than European cultural and political life.[9] In their moral absolutism, their support for censorship of language or image they deem 'inappropriate' and their belief in state regulation of private behaviour, such movements bear an ironic resemblance to the Christian Right at its fundamentalist extreme. Indeed, it is tempting to see politically correct ideology as a form of counter-fundamentalism. So similar in character are political correctness and Protestant fundamentalism, however, that it may be more useful to see them as products of the same culture. The old prohibitions, vehemently defended by the 'moral majority', logically give way to the new prohibitions, imposed by the feminist movement, 'gay rights' and race relations bureaucrats. Thus Jeff's arguments for the banning of men's clubs, on classic politically correct grounds, appear identical to the arguments of old time moralists for the prohibition of homosexuality between consenting adults.[10] They represent cultural continuity, which is ironic, since one of the new liberalism's main tenets is contempt for history. Gore Vidal, who is at least as good a commentator as he is a novelist, suggested once that the Puritans did not come to America because they were being persecuted, but because they were not free to persecute anyone else. Political correctness, Puritanism's most recent manifestation in American life, appears to bear out his observation.

The Puritan ethos of political correctness is reflected in the obsessions of new liberals with sex and sexual morality, questions of which they place above economics, political theory and it seems all aspects of life. Politically correct sexual mores are based on a reversal of traditional strictures. The result is not genuine tolerance, or even the much-trumpeted new openness to which sexual radicals have aspired. Instead, political correctness leads to a set of new restrictions, less subtle but more rigorous and enforced with greater fervour than those sanctioned by tradition. Whereas the old Puritanism imposed straightforward prohibitions, the new Puritanism interprets sexual behaviour, morality and intimate relationships exclusively in terms of political 'rights' and the struggle to achieve 'equality'. Old-style moralists reduced conversation about sexual matters to hushed whispers, innuendo and condemnation. Politically correct moralists, by a similar process of censorship, reduce it to a form of cultural relativism in which 'anything goes' except for criticism of 'permissiveness' and any arrangement is acceptable, apart from traditional arrangements, which are inherently suspect. Thus the 'conventional family' is criticised as 'patriarchal', whilst same-sex marriages become a 'right' and the centre of a campaign. Under the pretext of 'sexual equality', politically correct Puritans seek to police male sexuality in the same way as traditional moralists policed female sexuality. The old Puritanism, based on prohibition, and the new Puritanism, based on 'rights', both increase levels of distrust between individuals and within society. Both reflect a profoundly negative attitude towards sex, connecting it with shame and fear, with purely physical actions or abstract political concepts, instead of relationships of affection and trust.

Like the old-style Puritan, the politically correct campaigner envisages the state and the law as agents of moral deliverance, shaping the private and public behaviour of the citizen. There is therefore a parallel between the proliferation of laws and moral regulations characteristic of Puritan societies and the earnest rigour underlying 'Equal Opportunities' edicts. When the enforcement of morals fails, the traditional Puritan's impulse is to pass new laws. When 'Equal Opportunities' provisions do not produce the desired outcome, the politically correct Puritan's impulse is also to legislate, create new codes of practice, devise new forms of 'discrimination' to combat with 'government action' and invent new group rights for activists to assert. In the Puritan colonies of North America, the range of sexual prohibitions enshrined in law was astonishingly varied and wide-ranging.[11] The United States today has a similarly bewildering array of anti-discrimination laws, in which a corps of professional activists, legal experts and bureaucrats place quasi-religious faith and enforce with Puritan enthusiasm.

Thus, in his desire to ban male clubs in the interests of 'anti-discrimination', Jeff is very much in the tradition of Puritans who sought to ban dancing in the interests of 'public morals'.[12] Politically correct Puritanism is by no means confined to the United States, although it is at its most virulent in North America, where it encounters less cultural resistance than in the older cultures of Europe. Nonetheless, it influences strongly the legislative agendas and structures of the European Union, largely because these structures lack strong historical roots and have no genuine connection with European culture – except, perhaps, for those elements in European thought that seek perfection and centralised uniformity. In Britain, which has a Puritan tradition of its own, the campaign against 'institutionalised racism' has most of the characteristics of a religious mania, with individuals and whole institutions 'confessing' their 'guilt' and pledging submission to further state control.[13] The myriad 'racism awareness', 'diversity training' and 'anti-sexist' programmes incorporated into education and government at the behest of politically correct campaigns bear a close resemblance to religious evangelism, in their dogmatic certainty, linguistic piety, appeal to emotion in place of clear thinking, and the threat of their legal sanctions against transgressors.

Understanding the Puritan heritage of political correctness also helps us to understand the extreme emotional rhetoric of feminist, gay rights and race relations activists. It gives a cultural context to their desire to impose their will on others, their wish to change human nature (using the state to do so) and their fanatical exhortations to members of 'their' constituent groups. Both the old and the new Puritanism place strong emphasis on social conformity and peer group pressure as ways to suppress 'unacceptable' opinions. They seek to change outward behaviour, but at the same time to alter the individual's inner life. At a time in England when Puritanism was gathering momentum, Queen Elizabeth I stated that it was not her aim as ruler to 'make window's into men's souls'. She said this, at once to reinforce her demand for outward religious conformity, authoritarian in modern terms, and to restrain the most extreme Protestants, who wanted to change the way people thought and behaved. 'Old' Puritanism and political correctness both aim to make windows into men's souls and, needless to say, the souls of women, too. They seek to police the language the individual uses[14] and 'reform' the way he organises his thoughts. It is not for nothing that 'thought crimes' were the most heinous offences in Orwell's *1984* and that 'thought reform' was the aim of re-education in Mao's China. These two totalitarian states, one fictional, one real, were deeply Puritanical in nature and have much in common with the social agenda of political correctness.

There are, nonetheless, significant differences between the political correctness of new liberals and the more traditional brand of Puritanism. First of all, the origins of the latter are religious, whereas the former is in essence a secular fundamentalism, although some of its adherents might profess religious beliefs. This difference affects in an important but subtle way the character of the two movements. For although it is prohibitive, collectivist and often extremely bigoted, the emphasis of religious Puritanism is still fundamentally upon the individual, or more specifically the individual's relationship with the Creator. The emphasis of political correctness, by contrast, is exclusively on the group. Similarly, although religious Puritans seek power and use it to impose their world-view, and although they are often highly materialistic and acquisitive, they also have other-worldly ambitions: for themselves, those they wish to 'save', and above all the community whose spiritual direction they seek to influence. Politically correct campaigners see secular power as a desirable end in itself, as well as a means to punish their opponents and pass laws to perpetuate their power.

In political correctness, there is little room, therefore, for the individual as a living, breathing man or woman, let alone a soul in need of salvation. Instead, politically correct activists set out to alter the individual's social attitudes and behaviour to make him more compliant or use him as an instrument of power. In my discussion with Jeff, he told me that homosexual members of my Club should be 'made to' confront their 'internalised homophobia' and should 'have to' show solidarity with lesbians, as well as the 'wider' feminist movement.[15] This might suggest a continuation of the Puritan emphasis of personal salvation. That element certainly does exist. Supporters of identity-based politics, such as Jeff, are frequently motivated by genuine concern for others. This quickly mutates into a desire to rescue them from 'wrong' thoughts. As with the Puritans of old, they doubt the capacity of individuals to form opinions for themselves and, for all their talk of diversity, flatly refuse to accept the idea of 'different strokes for different folks', or that solutions besides their own can work. Such personal concerns are subordinated to considerations of group identity. The recalcitrant individual is a problem not because he is in danger of 'damnation', but because his waywardness presents a threat to the group. His defiance, or indifference, to the demands of his would-be liberators undermines the activist power game. This is why it is important that he 'has to' conform and should be 'made to' change his behaviour and outlook.

Religious Puritanism, despite its restrictive practices, makes moral demands of the individual and strong appeals to personal responsibility. Political correctness, however, robs the individual of responsibility and demands that he subsume his personal identity in a group identity. Thus, for all its vicissitudes, religious Puritanism has more of a human scale than politically correct ideology. It flourishes in small communities, in regions[16] and nation-states. Although its influence is often censorious and stultifying, it can be modified or resisted at a variety of levels. These include national and state politics, or working through personal contacts at local level. Political correctness is an urban phenomenon best suited to large units of government, multinational states[17] or those metropolitan areas increasingly balkanised on ethnic, cultural or sexual lines.[18] Unlike Puritanism, it lacks any genuine popular base and so must be imposed from above upon an unwilling citizenry. Thus it is easier to mitigate the effects of religious Puritanism, or even persuade its adherents to change their minds, than it is to modify politically correct campaigns or persuade their activists to think again. Because Puritanism retains a degree of commitment to the individual, it can also have a humane and practical side, inspiring valuable social reforms such as better housing, access to education and health care, the extension of political participation, including the involvement of women. It can inspire individuals to acts of courage, good will and personal sacrifice, as well as appealing to a sense of community that transcends narrow materialism. This is why a veteran American socialist, interviewed by sociologist Betty Yorburg, expresses approval of some aspects of the Puritan tradition in the United States:

"I think morality in the United States is in a state of collapse. ... Our traditional morality, you know, for good or evil, is dying.

"And there are lots of things about the old morality that I like. There's a certain austerity in the Puritan tradition that I like.

"I think that a certain kind of purity, of Puritanism, is excellent – absolutely excellent!"[19]

These remarks were made to Dr Yorburg in the late 1960s, at a time when democratic socialism in America was all but dead and when, more generally in the West, the New Left's 'personal-is-political' ideology was challenging the communitarianism of the Old Left. Stalwarts of that Old Left still stressed the importance of communities, especially local communities, in improving the lot of ordinary people, bringing dignity and the chance of betterment to the poor. They emphasised the individual's obligation to others and the value of voluntary activity, in the charitable or cultural spheres, and of co-operative endeavours in economic matters. It was by these means, they believed, that true individual liberty was realised, because it was indivisible from the idea of social responsibility. Individual liberty existed within a civil society that was genuinely inclusive, not balkanised into interest groups. The function of government, whether local or national, was to facilitate reform. In direct opposition to these principles, the New Left promoted a politics of self-gratification for individuals and a consumerist idea of rights or entitlements for groups.

Although New Leftists tried to co-opt the language of communitarianism, inventing phrases like 'black community' and 'gay community' that now trip off politically correct tongues, their emphasis was on fragmenting civil society, dissolving traditional communities (including the working-class communities that gave Old Left socialism its power base) and abolishing all obligations between individuals that might seem to impose restraints. With the emergence of the 1960s New Left came the marked shift of emphasis from economic to social issues, from settled values to an atmosphere of moral chaos that provided the cultural background to political correctness. The New Left's emphasis on sexual liberation and related issues did not point in the direction of radical economic change. Whilst its adherents denounced consumer-capitalism, they provided the me-first society with a new type of ethical underpinning. The radical wing of the Old Left, including orthodox Communists, were well aware of the problems posed by the new radical generation, with its increasingly assertive 'politics of ecstasy'. They knew that the unprincipled hedonism and uncontrolled rebellion of the times made serious revolutionary change less probable:

> Allurements to ecstasy and revolutionary propaganda … make good bedfellows for disrupting society, though … the more serious and organised revolutionary movements, which not only aim to overthrow society but plan to substitute a new order which they can themselves control, will have none of it, and are often almost Victorian in their moral standpoints. This gives a further pointer to the swing of young revolutionary fashions from orthodox Communism to less boring and more succulent alternatives.[20]

As its campaigns hardened gradually into militant identity politics, the New Left damaged moderate as much as orthodox revolutionaries.

It also developed its own narrow orthodoxies. These found political expression in a form of counter-morality whereby everything that was tried, tested and stable was 'repressive', whatever its human value. There could be no objective discussion of this counter-morality, because to discuss objectively was a form of repression, as was rational thought itself, or opposition to slogans that reduced and simplified human experience. This approach is encapsulated in the following extract from the work of a British academic, taken from an otherwise thoughtful critique of Tony Blair's New Labour administration and its acceptance of free-market ideology:

> A positive gloss is put on virtually every aspect of the government's activities. However, what is referred to here as positive largely relates to traditional and conventional family-orientated values. Homosexuality, single-parenthood, alternative lifestyles and many other things are either ignored, confined to the periphery of political concern **or even criticized.** Thus the stereotype of deviancy is reinforced. Jack Straw, as Home Secretary [1997-2001], **apparently thought it completely acceptable to voice his 'personal opinion'** of opposition to adoption by lesbians and gay men and lesbian IVF [in-vitro fertilisation] mothers in November 1997. Likewise with the concentration on, and scapegoating of, single parents and asylum seekers. All these reinforce the ignorance and prejudices of sections of the population and are, thus, emotional in nature.[21] *[My emphases.]*

As is customary with such expositions of the new liberalism, there is a roll call of labels and classifications, which tend to be arbitrary and inaccurate. Since most single parents, mothers especially, are not single by choice, their situation can hardly be likened to 'alternative lifestyles', a vague and unhelpful phrase the definition of which appears to be of little interest to the author. Equally misleading is the phrase 'lesbians and gay men', given the contrasting, indeed conflicting, natures of male and female homosexuals. There is also a distinctly dictatorial tone, a disapproval of legitimate 'criticism' or discussion. In his apparent contempt for 'traditional and conventional family-orientated forms and values', the author elevates unconventional, anti-family forms and values to the level of politically correct sacred cows. More apparent than anything else, however, is the underlying callousness of the author's approach. Unlike the Home Secretary, whose 'personal opinion' is deemed illegitimate, he does not care about children forced to grow up without fathers, or born to 'unconventional' unions through the misguided intervention of medical science. He appears to regard adoption as a reasonable vehicle for social experiment, although the objects of experiment are usually the most vulnerable children. He also appears indifferent to the plight of single mothers living on low income, struggling to raise their children alone and frequently displaying great dignity and courage, but wishing their circumstances were different. This is not because the author himself lacks compassion. In much of his book, he castigates New Labour for its uncompassionate economic policies and for continuing the Thatcherite project in a disguised form. The glib ideological categories of political correctness deaden compassionate instincts. They destroy the capacity to see human beings. There are no individuals, only 'single mothers', 'lesbians and gay men' or 'alternative lifestyles'. Their problems are not individual but abstract. For new liberals, ultimately, it is the *im*personal that is political.

The ideology of new liberalism inherits from the 1960s 'radical generation' a hostility to family structures and communities of a 'traditional and conventional' type. It equates family breakdown with personal freedom and sexual emancipation, ignoring the emotional deprivation, loneliness and poverty that such developments have brought, as well as the long-term cost in terms of social dislocation and crime. In the United States, for example, the link between future criminal behaviour or drug addiction in young men and growing up in a single-mother household has been seen to be statistically higher than any other sociological linkage, including ethnicity and economic class.[22] The cost of the breakdown of 'traditional and conventional family forms' pervades Western society, particularly the English-speaking world, but disproportionately affects the poor. It also disproportionately affects women and some ethnic minorities and so would appear to be highly 'politically incorrect'. Family breakdown, and the more general assault on custom and structure in the name of 'rights', is being shown to have an especially detrimental effect on boys and young men. They often find themselves bereft of adequate male role models at home and – with increasing frequency – at school. In their education they are constrained by a 'feminised' curriculum that fails to offer them practical training or take account of their emotional needs. Deprived of a rite of passage, and the opportunity to learn from the experience of older men, youths who are already from disadvantaged backgrounds are more likely to become dangerous to themselves and others, to grow up into absent fathers or violent partners, or at the very least remain in a state of protracted adolescence. New liberals, despite inheriting from Marxists a desire to make connections between areas of human activity, dogmatically fail to connect the structural assault on family and community with the emergence of a violent underclass, the proliferation of neuroses and mental disorders amongst the more affluent, or the dehumanising, stressful conditions of so much of urban life. In this respect, new liberals show themselves to be as blind and doctrinaire as the 'hangers and floggers' of the right.

What appears to be extreme individualism turns out therefore to be yet another means by which political correctness undermines individual identity. Taken together, the increasing dissolution of the family, the abolition of rites of passage for young men and civilised aspirations for young women[23], the demotion of motherhood as a social institution[24] and the denial of any spiritual dimension to human life all discourage the development of mature, rounded human beings. This 'revaluation of all values', engendered by the late twentieth century variant of liberalism lacks the lofty, exalted qualities that Nietzsche associated with the phrase when he used it to describe his questioning philosophy. Instead, its implications are at once sordid and banal and they extend well beyond family structures. As moral obligations are eroded in the more intimate areas of life, so other forms of loyalty are called into question. These include the relationship of trust (such as it was) between employer and employee, the notion of shared citizenship, transcending differences of income, region, race or class, along with any notions of restraint, good manners and even tolerance itself, however much new liberals extol the latter virtue. For if relationships between human beings are characterised by moral ambiguity, with no clear underlying values, then political and economic responsibilities become similarly ambiguous. Insecurity therefore becomes increasingly the norm in employment as well as the family, with change replacing continuity as the dominant theme of public and private aspects of life.

Rapid and unpredictable technological changes have contributed to this *fin-de-siecle* age of anxiety, just as advances in reproductive technology made possible the sexual revolution of the late twentieth century. Both these developments bring with them new possibilities for positive change as well as confusion and insecurity. Communications technology can increase our choice of where we live and how we work, freeing millions of human beings from degrading labour, benefiting small businesses, the self employed and local economies. Reproductive technology can benefit men, women and families, providing genuine liberation from poverty and fear. Paradoxically, such positive changes cannot usefully take place without a background of stability and continuity. The assault on 'traditional and conventional' moral structures in the name of cultural revolution has generated fear and uncertainty instead of constructive reform. Moral relativism has spread from the personal and sexual to the economic sphere. The notion of 'the personal as political' has evolved into the idea that 'there is no such thing as society', a doctrine underlying free-market fundamentalism. Far from ushering in a more just, or even freer, society, the New Left's attack on cultural tradition was the harbinger of a revived market dogma, whose partisans have attacked social obligation with the same ardour as the liberal-left attack on 'old-fashioned' morals. Both movements complement and reinforce each other, pointing towards a less secure, increasingly nihilistic society. This convergence is by no means historically unprecedented. Alexis de Tocqueville's account of the French Revolution and its origins shows how certain sceptical, but strangely uncritical, philosophical movements undermined social stability and eventually liberty itself, by their intemperate assault on everything tried and tested. Tocqueville draws our attention in particular to two philosophical movements that laid the foundations for the modern cult of the market and which were also, in the context of their age, intensely politically correct:

> Towards the middle of the eighteenth century a group of writers known as the "Physiocrats" or "Economists", who made the problems of public administration their special study, came on the scene. …Whereas the philosophers depicted imaginary utopias, the Economists sometimes pointed out what could and should be done in the existing world. Their chief targets of attack were those institutions which the Revolution was destined to sweep away forever; not one of them found favour in their eyes. Those, on the other hand, which we regard as creations of the Revolution were anticipated and warmly advocated by them. Indeed, the germinal ideas of practically all the permanent changes effected by the Revolution can be found in their works.

> What is more, their writings had the democratic-revolutionary tenor characteristic of so much modern thought. **For they attacked not only**

specific forms of privilege but any kind of diversity whatsoever; to their thinking all men should be equal even if equality spelled servitude, and every obstacle to the achievement of this end should be done away with immediately. For contractual engagements they had no respect, and no concern for private rights. Indeed, private rights were, in their eyes, negligible; only the public interest mattered. Though most of them were amiable, well-meaning persons, men of substance, conscientious public servants or administrators, such was their enthusiasm for the cause they sponsored that they carried their theories to fanatical lengths.

Our Economists had a vast contempt for the past. "The nation has been governed," Letronne declared, "on wrong lines altogether; one has the impression that everything was left to chance". Starting out from this premise, they set to work, and there was no French institution, however venerable and well founded, for whose immediate suppression they did not clamour for if it hampered them to even the slightest extent or did not fit in with their neatly ordered scheme of government. ...

It is a curious fact that when they envisaged all the social and administrative reforms subsequently carried out by our revolutionaries, the idea of free institutions never crossed their minds. True, they were all in favour of the free exchange of commodities and a system of laissez faire and laissez passer in commerce and industry; but political liberty in the full sense of the terms was something that passed their imagination or was promptly dismissed from their thoughts if by any chance the idea of it occurred to them.[25] [My emphases.]

In these two movements, with their thoroughly modern ideals of 'progress' as an end in itself, we see clearly the symbiosis between the indiscriminate dismantling of traditional structures, the rise of 'each man for himself' economics and, paradoxically perhaps, the rise of the state. The Economists and Physiocrats, after all, opposed all forms of hierarchical structure, benevolent as well as reactionary, all institutions and practices that had evolved over time, whether they were repositories of unjust privilege or guarantors of security. This revolt against tradition, throwing out the good with the bad, was because the very idea of tradition conflicted with their abstract commitment to equal rights. Like the free-market enthusiasts of today, they opposed all 'feudal' constraints on the accumulation of wealth and looked upon economic growth as the supreme value. But they shared with today's new liberals a belief in the state as the agent of change, the rigid enforcer of 'Equal Opportunities', but not opportunities tailored to individuals. Like modern political correctness, their ideology had little place for the individual, except as an economic unit or the supposed beneficiary of charters of rights. They believed in structures into which individuals must fit and laws with which they must comply. For Economists and Physiocrats, there was no place for local custom, eccentricity or anomaly, no place indeed for personal choice, if such things conflicted with their ideal of rational humanity. Like my politically correct dinner companion, they would almost certainly have banned men's clubs. They would have shared his abstract abhorrence of 'discrimination', his belief in group rights in place of individual freedom and his support for the intrusive state – as long as its intrusions took place in the name of 'progress'.

In their secular crusade against tradition, and their elevation of commercial over human values, the *littérateurs* of the pre-Revolutionary epoch provided a rationale for the Terror that shortly ensued. Dictatorship in the name of liberty was the Terror's main precept, whilst the pursuit of absolute Reason justified unreasoned bloodletting. The ideological affinity between the 'progressive' musings of Economists and the reign of Jacobin terror are clear enough. More subtly, however, the undermining of historical precedent and custom over the fifty years preceding the Revolution robbed political life of any consistency. It created a climate of moral relativism in which any action appeared permissible if it served some ill-defined ultimate goal. Furthermore, the wholesale abandonment of tradition meant that the structures mediating between the individual and the state were all eroded or destroyed. These include political and religious institutions, voluntary associations (such as clubs) and 'traditional or conventional' mores that restrain individual excess and provide some guidance in the conduct of human affairs. The state filled the ethical and emotional vacuum and assumed a power far more sweeping than that of the Ancien Regime.

The new liberalism presents us with some similar problems. Its adherents, like Toccqueville's idealistic 'littérateurs', allow little room for human variety. Their ceaseless talk of diversity is forked-tongued, for under the rubric of political correctness, they seek to impose a uniformity of behaviour and thought. New liberals do not appreciate true diversity. They place abstract principles before real human need, regarding those principles as universally valid and beyond question. As a result, they put their faith in laws and structures, erected by the state or imposed by court ruling, regarding local initiatives and voluntary activities with great suspicion. One of the Economists whom Tocqueville decried 'proposed the abolition of all the existing territorial divisions of France and the renaming of the provinces'.[26] In our present age, his new liberal successors champion the abolition of nation-states and their replacement by supranational entities whose powers they seek to increase.[27] In the context of federations, such as the United States, they favour the federal power over the principle of states rights. Small businesses, craftsmen and independent farmers are also natural enemies of the new liberal, who favours large-scale units, be they state or corporate.

Whereas traditional liberalism has strong local roots, new liberalism is a centralising force, prepared to coerce instead of persuade. Its commitment to political correctness blocks off the possibility of local variation and prevents consideration of individual needs. Opponents of political correctness should not be lulled into complacency by the absence of an immediate revolutionary drama. The corrosion of values is if anything more insidious than a sudden cataclysm, because the sense of freedom and responsibility is lost gradually, whilst the process of intellectual surrender is protracted and covert.

3. The Liberal Surrender

Some years ago, when I was a schoolboy and the phrase political correctness was, as far as I know, unheard of, I picked up a magazine in the dentist's waiting room. I think it was *Punch*, which at that time combined genuine wit with astute social comment. One of the cartoon strips, I recall, immediately amused and delighted me, for it retold, as a modernist parody, the story of 'Goldilocks and the Three Bears'. In the cartoon, a plaited, solemn-looking social worker named Goldie Lox wanders into a house on a 'sink' estate and noses around amongst the family's possessions. Suddenly, the tenants return and surprise her with their ursine appearance. But level-headed, unprejudiced and uncompromisingly modern, Ms Lox has a ready response: " Ah, bears. You must celebrate your ethnic identity."

That was Britain in the late 1970s. I was only tentatively aware of politics, largely because they were discussed at home and the news was never missed. My view of society was not yet formed, although I had rejected the hypocritical brand of Christian piety imposed by my prep school's Headmaster, itself a stifling prototype of politically correct dogma. Indeed, if I owe anything to this man at all, it is a scepticism and hatred of cant, although he taught me this quite unintentionally. At that time, the phrase 'ethnic minorities' was entering popular political discourse. The Commission for Racial Equality was beginning its work and was concerned, for the most part, with finding practical solutions to racial injustice, rather than calling for 'positive discrimination' or trying to impose a state ideology of 'multiculturalism'. More ideological were the overwhelmingly middle-class Anti-Nazi League protesters, who relished violent clashes with the racist and overwhelmingly working-class National Front.

These self-styled anti-racists – some of whom were already becoming teachers or social workers like Goldie Lox – were Marxists of sorts, usually Trotskyites, which meant that unlike orthodox Communists they did not have to apologise for the Soviet Union since 1927.[1] Their standard response to criticism of 'really existing socialist' regimes, such as the former East Germany and the Soviet Union, was (and is) to blame Stalin for 'what went wrong', a curiously 'personalist' approach for professed social determinists.[2] In any case, the anti-racist crusaders approached the white, working-class populations of inner cities with the arrogance and bad faith characteristic of the worst sort of colonial missionaries. The working-class were benighted natives, in need of rescue from their antiquated prejudices. In general, the 'anti-Nazi' demonstrators were regarded as violent and obnoxious, as bad as the far right parties they allegedly opposed but in truth relied upon.

At that time, I knew about these left-right clashes, because I watched them in the news and was beginning to read about them in the paper.[3] But I knew nothing of 'ethnic minorities'. Although I had amongst my school friends and my parents' acquaintance people from all over the world, it never occurred to me to think of them as belonging to minority or majority populations, still less to separate 'communities' with special needs. Indeed it had never occurred to me to treat them as anything other than individuals, with virtues or faults like anybody else. There were cultural differences, which aroused in me interest and curiosity; they worshipped different gods and sometimes had different ethical codes. To me, this made no difference: I respected their cultures and they respected mine.

That was, perhaps, my eleven year-old notion of equality, which I probably would not have called equality but fairness, a word I continue to prefer. I knew that racial prejudice was personally hurtful and morally disreputable – from whatever source it came. When I was younger, my mother had given me a book from America called *Black Like Me*, in which a white, Northern journalist named John Howard Griffin had, through medical treatment, temporarily darkened his skin.[4] This enlightening experiment took place in the American South, before desegregation and civil rights, and so for a middle-class white man the consequences of changing colour were horrendous. *Black Like Me* was a compelling, often shocking catalogue of insults, cruelty and humiliation, with occasional instances of goodness that redeem the reader's faith in humanity. The book is a more effective inoculation against racial prejudice than any government-inspired report. It is certainly far superior to the multicultural propaganda tracts introduced in state schools by 'progressive' educational authorities and teachers – with the acquiescence, through fear, of conservatives and liberals in the educational world. This is because it is about the complex and varied experiences of an individual, related as part of a plea for other individuals. It is about the emancipation of people, black and white, as individual human beings, instead of a call for abstract rights for arbitrarily defined groups.

Of course, I would not have used a phrase like 'abstract rights' at that age. All that came later. Why, then, was I so diverted by the waiting room cartoon that I remember it to this day? Looking back, I believe that I might have understood more about politics than I realised. For, although political correctness had yet to embed itself in public policy, this was a time of transition. The assumptions, political and economic, underlying the post-war consensus were rapidly crumbling. In the economic sphere, the principle of public ownership of utilities was under two-pronged attack, at one level from a resurgent free-market fundamentalism, at another from an assortment of New Left radicals, within the Labour Party and outside it, as well as Marxists of a more conventional stamp. Then, as now, such radicals punched above their weight. They enjoyed negligible public support, but compensated for this by a compulsive activism that gave them disproportionate prominence within trade unions, academic institutions and single-issue campaigns.

The programme of nationalisation, introduced by the Labour government of 1945-51, had created increasingly sclerotic industries and public service, bloated and inefficient management structures and appalling Labour relations. Nationalised industries, in other words, appeared to be fulfilling the worst predictions of Sir Richard Acland, leader of Common Wealth and its only post-war MP. Common Wealth was a small party that combined a libertarian and decentralised form of socialism with the attempt to apply genuine Christian principles to politics. Common Wealth received considerable support from servicemen who had been radicalised by wartime activity. For large parts of the War, it was the only effective opposition force, when the Conservative, Liberal and Labour parties – and the Communists, also[5] – agreed not to stand against each other. Despite winning several by-elections during the early 1940s and enjoying respect across the political spectrum, the movement petered out quickly when the war ended. In 1946, its leader summed up his objections to the Labour Party's economic programme in these terms:

> Nationalisation falls short of socialisation in two vital respects. First, it fails to establish vital democracy in industry, making no provision for workers' control and inadequate provision for consumer control. Secondly, it leaves the wage system intact and makes little or no advance towards that economic quality essential to socialists.
>
> ... Other differences relate to the Labour Party policy of compensation to dispossessed capitalists, and to the tempo of its advance towards even public ownership. A government calling itself socialist is in fact administering capitalism – and this involves serious risk. By removing the harsh discipline of the employer by various means, including social insurance, it is reducing the old incentives to hard work. At the same time, by leaving private ownership largely intact and by giving no measure of industrial democracy even in nationalised industries, it is failing to provide new socialist incentives. The low output figures per man-hour are acknowledged by responsible socialists and Labour leaders to be one of the brakes on Britain's industrial recovery, and the Labour Government's destruction of old incentives without the creation of new is a factor contributing to that low output. This is one of Labour's most vulnerable points, and failure here might bring irremediable disaster.[6]

State monoliths, in short, replicate all the worst features of capitalism. However they also remove the element of individual creativity that can, on occasion, humanise a free market system. In place of the market, they put only a stifling, bureaucratic conformity. In the Common Wealth pamphlet, the reference to 'consumer control' has a curiously late twentieth century ring. The hostility to compensating 'dispossessed capitalists' is both unjust and wrongheaded, signifying one of the flaws in most socialist movements, a propensity for collective punishment.[7] Common Wealth was, nonetheless, the most humane and individualistic of socialist movements, grounded in a peculiarly British tradition of free-thinking now almost wholly absent from political debate.

The Common Wealth critique of nationalisation holds up an alternative view of common ownership, in which it is quite compatible with good workmanship, good service to customers, choice for worker and consumer alike. Above all, it aims to reconcile socialism with decentralisation and individual freedom. Had this approach influenced a broader section of the British left, it might have proved a valuable inoculation against the 'group rights' ideologies of multiculturalism and 'gender' feminism, both largely imported from the United States, as well as the strident sub-Marxist bigotry of the 1960s New Left. There might never have been a resurgence of market fundamentalism, with its indiscriminate hostility to public provision. Or, at the very least, the left might have countered the claims of free-market ideologues with a more human-scale, more reassuring vision of society. In the 1970s, the moderate left had failed to transcend a narrow, state-focused economic philosophy. At the same time, it was surrendering intellectually and culturally to extremists, with their oft-repeated incantations against 'racism' and 'sexism' – isms with which the whole of Western civilisation was allegedly tainted.

By failing to adopt human-scale economics or face down a new breed of Puritan bigotry, the left lost any vision of civil society that it had previously possessed. Conservatives were similarly discarding most notions of common endeavour, embracing a bogus form of individualism by which human beings are reduced to economic units and the measure of all things is economic growth, not quality of life. Gone were the 'little platoons' of Edmund Burke's conservatism, those who held community life together, often by voluntary activities. Just as the left aimed to replace them with state officials, the new right aimed to replace them with businessmen. The liberal tradition in Britain characterised by tolerance, a sense of individual liberty and a belief in social justice had been losing its intellectual momentum for some time. Distinctions between that form of liberalism and the group-based ideologies of the New Left were blurring quickly by the time I saw the *Punch* cartoon.

By then, liberal intellectuals were failing so manifestly to defend traditional notions of freedom and responsibility, still less adapt them to changing times, that they seemed to be little more than reassuring mouthpieces for the cultural radicals. The betrayal of freedom by *bien pensant* liberals laid the foundations for politically correct hegemony, because it removed a powerful source of intellectual resistance. From the 1960s onwards, the marriage of liberal and New Left interests (with the latter in full control) has ensured that authoritarian collectivism becomes the dominant political model, in place of individual freedom and an inclusive civil society.[8] In their trenchant analysis of student and academic disruption at the Polytechnic of North London (PNL), three academics living through the troubles describe the difficulties confronted by many liberal lecturers (and more than a few students) and their surrender to radical collectivism. *Rape of Reason*, the account of events at PNL[9] produced by Keith Jacka, Caroline Cox and John Marks, is of historical importance as well as political value. It marks a depressing chapter in the history of ideas, records a frenzied assault on the principles of academic freedom and points to political and cultural trends that are central to our discussion:

> The manipulators have been successful because the natural guardians of the academy, i.e. the liberals, have capitulated. They have given up in the face of the liberal dilemma. Their failure was inevitable in that they persisted in playing the game by the rules, while the radicals blatantly did not. ...
>
> In an academy the 'liberals' are by far the biggest group. But they are also the most confused and ambivalent in their attitudes to authority. In a crisis of academic government they split into pro- and anti-administration. The pro-admin 'liberals', after a period of observation and indecision, see the radicals as a major threat to the values of the academy and of liberal democracy, and therefore swing to the defence of the administration. They have been few at PNL. The anti-admin 'liberals', uncritically swayed by the same sacred topics as the young radicals (e.g. racism), find it too painful to revise the category of innocent youth fighting for a better world. They cannot exchange this for the more realistic but more bitter category of the smug and arrogant simplifiers, or the category of cynical young manipulators. Rather than abandon their original category, they prefer to edit the facts.
>
> Many 'liberals' believe that the administration should always manoeuvre to avoid confrontation; hence the mere existence of conflict is evidence of administrative failure. This gives the radicals both a large advantage and a strong motive for initiating conflict. ... The anti-admin 'liberals', numerous at PNL, retain their old style and their unexamined prejudice – a reflex distrust of authority, a glamorising of youth, and a predilection for 'progressive' change – regardless of the fundamental principles of an academy. Even if they have private doubts about some actions of the radicals, rarely in the prevailing intimidatory atmosphere do they have the courage or integrity to express them publicly.[10]

Since that time, the intimidatory atmosphere has spread beyond higher education and the student movement to much of the public sector, including primary and secondary education, social services and, significantly, the police and most areas of the Armed Forces. Increasingly, it dictates the language of politics and the media, constrains cultural discourse and creates an increasingly impoverished and cliché-ridden intellectual climate. Many private businesses, charities and voluntary organisations have been similarly 'intimidated', to the extent that their language, their structures and their attitudes towards the individual resemble those of New Left radicals.

The equivocating liberal academicians whose established a pattern followed by senior civil servants, senior military officers, the legal profession and mainstream politicians in the years that followed. Underlying this process of surrender is a failure to defend and clarify the liberal world-view. This failure, as we have seen, arises out of a loss of confidence in liberal values and a loss of belief in the very civilisation that inspired them. The protection of individual freedom is no longer seen as, in itself, a worthwhile purpose of government. Freedom of speech and freedom of association are not valued as ends in themselves, nor as indicators of a civilised society. Indeed both formerly liberal ideals are looked upon with suspicion by the new breed of collectivist liberal. The former is suspect because it includes the freedom to criticise cherished new orthodoxies, the latter because it can conflict with the principle of rigid, enforceable 'equality'. 'Equality' is defined less in terms of equality of all individuals before the law, another traditionally liberal goal, and still less in terms of establishing a fair distribution of wealth. Instead, equality has come to be seen in terms of breaking the population into groups and distributing collective rights at the behest of self-appointed lobbyists. Such groups are defined by race, sex and other criteria that highlight differences between individuals. Yet true to forked-tongue form, the new liberal war cry is still 'integration'.

One of the contradictions at the heart of the new liberalism is that it is at once assimilationist and separatist in character. In both their ideological statements and their practical programmes, new liberals seek simultaneously to banish difference and to reinforce it. For example, the proposition that 'men and women are equal in every respect' has, since the 1970s at least, become an article of faith for those who wish to be considered 'progressive'. Men and women who dare challenge this shibboleth risk being accused of 'sexism'. Yet it is equally 'progressive' to speak uncritically about 'female perspectives' on politics or, like one otherwise excellent American ecological thinker, describe 'corporate and military hierarchies' as 'masculine forms of power', the implication being that 'masculine' means oppressive and reactionary, like 'bourgeois' or 'capitalist' in the vocabulary of vulgar Marxism.[11] Similarly, 'all races are equal' or 'all cultures are equally valid' are no longer considered by 'liberals' to be propositions open to challenge. However this should not be taken to mean that all individuals are equal in the eyes of the law, regardless of race, religion or colour. On the contrary, 'racial equality' includes the concept of 'hate crime', whereby an attack on a man because of his skin colour is more serious than an attack on him because he is bald or blue-eyed. Likewise, the equal validity of all cultures does not exempt 'non-white' communities from being censured for 'sexism' and 'homophobia'.

At one level, differences between races and cultures or biological differences between men and women mean nothing. At another, they are crucial components of political identity and the basis for political struggle. It is this paradox that gives rise to a forked-tongued political thinking. Instead of a clear line of argument, as in traditional liberal thought, there are two arguments running alongside each other and appearing to cancel each other out. Women are equal to men and yet possess superior insights and deserve special consideration. All races are 'equal' and yet some deserve more legal protection than others. Homosexuality, also, becomes at once a 'natural' phenomenon and a form of quasi-political rebellion. For liberals, old and new, laws based on religious and moral prejudice are inherently unjust, because a small percentage of men are homosexual by nature. Such thinking underlay the humanitarian reforms of the 1960s. Today, it gives credence to the more revolutionary agenda of 'gay rights'. This stipulates that heterosexuals and homosexuals have wholly identical interests. From this proposition, it follows that *any* legal differences between homosexual and heterosexual behaviour 'discriminate' and for that alone are beyond the pale. Homosexuality is natural behaviour for some men, and yet according to gay liberationist thinking (influenced by radical feminism), biology (i.e. nature!) has nothing to do with it. Sexual orientation is a product of the 'gender system', which – like the class system for Marxists – has to be overthrown:

... The oppressed position of gay people in so many societies is ulti-mately dependent on their deviation from the polarised gender stereo-types of masculine and feminine, **in which women are also oppressed by men.**

... The liberation of gay people is only possible as the liberation of homosexuality in general, and this in turn is possible only in the context of a breakdown of the gender system.[12] [*my emphases*]

And so, whilst some men are homosexual 'by nature', yet homo-sexuality and heterosexuality are both products of nurture, or 'the gender system'. In gay rights ideology, there is no such thing as 'gay' and 'straight' and yet individuals are routinely classified in those terms. Heterosexuality is a 'dominant culture', rather than the natural emotional and sexual state for most men and women. As such, it deserves no special consideration. Its 'privileges', again like class priv-ileges, should be 'challenged' and overthrown. Heterosexuality and homosexuality are 'equal', and yet:

Gay shows the way. In some ways we are **already** more advanced than straight people. We are already outside the family and we have already, in part at least, rejected the 'masculine' and 'feminine' roles society has designed for us. In a society dominated by the sexist culture, it is very dif-ficult, if not impossible, for heterosexual men and women to escape their rigid gender-role structuring and the roles of oppressor and oppressed. But gay men don't need to oppress women in order to fulfil their own psycho-sexual needs, and gay women [*sic*] don't have to relate sexually to the male oppressor, so that at this moment in time, the freest and most equal relationships are most likely to be between homosexuals.[13]

This passage is a good illustration of group rights ideology. It demonstrates also the way in which ideas once confined to a radical fringe have penetrated mainstream politics. For it is now quite com-monplace for homosexual activists – along with feminists and 'ethnic minority' campaigners – to assert their superiority to white, male or heterosexual cultures. In such ideological posturing, there is the same doublethink that George Orwell found characteristic of revolution-aries. As in the revolutionary climate of *Animal Farm*, all categories are equal, 'but some are more equal than others'. In the totalitarian atmosphere of *1984*, ignorance is transformed into a strength and slavery equated with freedom. Advocates of group rights promote 'diversity' but demand conformity, both in behaviour and thought. They espouse equality, but when they acquire power they impose an alternative hierarchy of privilege and entitlement as prescriptive as traditional class barriers. Thus all-male groups become 'discriminatory' and all-female groups 'empowering'. White-only groups become taboo, whereas black-only groups become an instrument of 'liberation'. Integration, racial and sexual, is to be forced on white Europeans and men respectively. Ethnic minorities and women, by contrast, should be encouraged to 'celebrate' their identities – and if they don't celebrate, they are betraying 'their' race or sex. 'Homophobia' becomes the third deadly sin (after racism and sexism), but 'gay pride' and the critique of the traditional family are articles of faith for activist homosexuals – those who refuse to take part are condemned as closeted.

In 'progressive' politics, group identity is defined as rigidly as caste came to be in later Hindu society. The New Left believes in a caste system from which the individual cannot escape, even when he wishes to do so. He (or she – for women are also a caste) is defined by racial or sexual characteristics that are supposed to influence his political behaviour.[14] When they do not do so, the fault lies with the individual, not with those supposedly promoting his or her 'rights'. This is why politically correct pressure groups often adopt a self-righteous, evangelical tone towards members of 'their' interest group who are ungrateful or refuse to co-operate. The practice by some gay rights groups of 'outing' their homosexual opponents is a good example of this, as is the disdain that many feminists show towards women who 'fail' to share their ideals. As the American philosopher Christina Hoff Sommers complains:

> Gender feminists are especially disapproving of the lives of traditionally religious women …, whom they see as being conditioned for highly restricted roles. Surely, they say, it is evident that such women are subjugated, and the choices they make inauthentic. As [well-known American feminist] Gloria Steinem explains it, "the appeal of [traditional religion] for women is that the promise is safety in return for obedience, respectability in return for self-respect and freedom – a sad bargain".
>
> This is a harsh judgement to make about millions of American women. Ms. Steinem is of course free to disagree with conventionally religious women on any number of issues, but she is not morally free to cast

aspersions on their autonomy and self-respect....The traditionally religious women of today, be they Protestant Christians, Orthodox Jews, or observant Catholics – emphatically do not think of themselves as subjugated, lacking in self-respect or unfree. Indeed, they very properly resent being described in that way. ... If they choose to lead the lives they do, that is their affair[15].

Professor Hoff Sommers is a fearless combatant on the side of traditional liberalism. Here, as elsewhere in her writings, she defends the principle of freedom for individuals within a civil society that offers a range of choices and possibilities and accepts a variety of beliefs and ways of life, as long as they are pursued peacefully and with respect for others. Politically correct campaigners, by contrast, do not believe in choice, although they use it as a slogan when appealing for traditional liberal support. Or, more precisely, they believe in choice for themselves but the denial of choice to their opponents. For if they have the 'right' to represent ethnic minorities, women or homosexuals, they cannot permit members of those groups to refuse to acknowledge their authority. If society is to be remoulded into 'alternative' castes, and the new caste system is to be the basis of politics, then it follows that there can be no dissent, no room for ambiguity.

Tolerance itself is no longer regarded as a political virtue by progressive opinion. On the contrary, it is politically suspect or incorrect. The demand for tolerance can be used as a lever against the 'majority culture' and as a way of softening up liberal opinion, but to the interest-group activist it is never reciprocal. Indeed, if he is tolerant towards his opponents, he is displaying weakness. In forked-tongued politics, tolerance can be demanded of others and at the same time systematically denied. The underlying truth is that tolerance is not valued, because it is incompatible with dogmatic activism and allows for differences between individuals and genuine, rather than politically charged, differences between groups. It allows for differences of opinion and shades of meaning, casting a shadow of doubt over politically correct slogans.

Tolerance allows for the questioning of cherished assumptions, be they 'conservative' or 'progressive' in nature. Politically, it points towards moderation rather than radicalism, a balance between conservation and change and a restraining sense of doubt instead of a zealous certainty. The activist therefore regards tolerance as a nuisance and a threat. It is worse than overt repression because it can expose the limitations of his thinking and expose him as unrepresentative of those he wishes to 'liberate'. Worse still, tolerant debate is likely to expose him to ridicule as the disconnectedness between his ideology and the needs of real human beings becomes more apparent. This is why the politically correct activist supports censorship of ideas he finds 'offensive' (i.e. challenging his certainties) and why he decries the liberal ethic of tolerance whenever he is confident enough to do so. The authors of *Rape of Reason* identify the attack on tolerance and free speech as an advanced symptom of the academy's decay:

> In [*the Polytechnic of North London*] there is also a correct line on Women's Liberation. In February 1974, in a series of open meetings, there was a pro-Women's Lib speaker one week followed by Arianna Stassinopoulos (anti-Women's Lib) the next. The first speaker had a warm reception, but not Miss Stassinopoulos. The ... Women's Lib group picketed the meeting and urged people not to attend. They failed to dissuade, so attended themselves in order to heckle. ... Later, during a heated exchange with a girl student, Miss Stassinopoulos asked her where in the world was there greater tolerance than in Britain. The girl replied: 'You are the one who counts tolerance as a good thing. I don't.'[16]

At the same time as these events at PNL, the National Union of Students Conference passed a motion enjoining student unions to 'take whatever measures are necessary ...to prevent any members of racialist or fascist organisations from speaking in colleges'.[17]

They also unsuccessfully attempted to introduce a list of 'banned books'. Later in 1974, Professor Samuel Huntington was prevented by student protesters from lecturing on the role of the United States military in foreign policy to Sussex University students and staff.[18] Justifying this action, the radical political scientist Anthony Arblaster claimed that 'free speech is only one value among many'.[19] The attempt to relativise free speech, by downgrading it from the cornerstone of a democratic and free society to one of many competing 'values', has been a more successful weapon against traditional liberal values than direct confrontation.

Examined closely, the idea of free speech as 'one value among many' is as absurd as it is dangerous. Force, after all, is also 'one value among many', as is censorship, as, for that matter, is racial prejudice. Yet the attack on freedom of speech has been central to the erosion of liberal values and the induction of liberals into collectivist patterns of thought. For *bien pensant* liberals today, opposing 'institutionalised racism' has come to be more important than free and open discussion. 'Gender equality' is placed above and beyond questioning and it is taken as read that an individual should be defined politically by his sexual orientation (and given the appropriate package of 'rights'). Because of the lack of convincing liberal resistance, these ideas have seeped from the extreme left to those who define themselves as liberals, to the extent that in the United States and increasingly in Britain the word 'liberal' is seen as a synonym for 'politically correct' – and so is associated with a closed system of thought instead of the belief in an open society. This is why we may speak of *authoritarian liberalism*. Authoritarian liberals regard politically correct values as the only authentic expression of freedom, and state- (or corporate-) imposed political correctness as the only way to make people free. To tolerate opposition is therefore to undermine freedom rather than enhance it. The attack on tolerance and free speech by self-professed liberals today has its roots in the New Left ideology that influenced the student protesters. Herbert Marcuse, the neo-Marxist philosopher who regarded 'bourgeois' freedom as an illusion, defined the traditionally liberal ethos of free expression as 'repressive tolerance'. He saw it as a force that undermined radical politics and so could not itself be tolerated.

Today's authoritarian liberals have absorbed this revolutionary world-view. They tend, increasingly, to see themselves as a political and cultural vanguard, whose superior knowledge entitles them to impose their ideas on an unwilling public. This explains another contradiction in political correctness. One of its central tenets is to be 'anti-elitist'. In the intellectual sphere, the 'anti-elitist' struggle matches the political struggles of anti-racism and anti-sexism. Elitism is, in politically correct terms, racist and sexist, because it is based – allegedly – on white and male notions of creativity, taste and advanced thought. Reason itself is suspect, because it is supposedly 'white' and 'male'. This assumption is a gross insult to reasoning women as well as ignoring the rationalist traditions of (for example) Indian, Chinese and Native American cultures. Forked-tongued politics is only 'inclusive' when it chooses to be. It therefore combines, without excessive self-consciousness, an 'anti-elitist' posturing with a belief, inherited from Leninism, that a political 'vanguard' is required to 'demystify the masses'.[20]

The more that politically correct assumptions increase their hold over intellectual life, the more remote intellectuals and their theories become from the experience of their fellow men and women. The discrepancy between politically correct theories about group behaviour and the choices real individuals make (irrespective of their 'groups') is more apparent as politically correct assumptions spread from the radical fringe to the mainstream of political and academic discourse. This is assumed to have a generally radicalising effect on society, by 'mainstreaming' fringe ideas to give them respectability and political clout. But as well as mainstreaming the fringe, political correctness 'fringes' the mainstream. It makes politics in general – rather than just extreme politics – more remote from and less interesting to the majority of citizens. It is no coincidence, then, that the rise of political correctness accompanies a decline in general interest in politics and democratic participation. The prevalence of group rights ideology amongst the 'political class' contrasts with the growing ridicule of such ideas amongst the wider public. The division between politics and people, or Political Man and Private Man, is widened by authoritarian liberalism, despite the claims of new liberals, already referred to above, to unite the personal with the political. In spite of their protestations of anti-elitism and identification with new social movements, politically correct campaigners have helped to create an increasingly closed, elitist political culture. It is not for nothing that 'liberal elite' has become a widespread term of political abuse.

Politically correct classifications, as we have noted, are applied with a rigidity akin to caste definitions. However caste, at least, allows for the possibility of rebirth, but as a materialistic, secular ideology, political correctness scorns other-worldly aspirations and scoffs at all spiritual solutions to the problems of individuals or mankind. For the individual cannot transcend the categories of race, sex and sexual orientation and should he try to do so, he is malevolent and dangerous. This does not stop attempts to 'reform' or 're-educate' perceived oppressors, through 'racism awareness courses' for white people (a form of racial discrimination in itself), or misguided efforts to impose 'feminine' values on men. Yet 'oppressed groups' are subject, under political correctness, to a crushing social determinism. Being 'black', female or 'gay' overrides individual identity, preference or taste.

Unlike caste, or class in Marxist definition, politically correct categories are rarely linked to occupation, economic status or even to culture. Caste and class have both (for good or ill) evolved organically. Therefore, they often play a critical role in shaping an individual's outlook on life, including his politics, work and spare-time activities. In the case of class in Western societies, this identification is sometimes negative. An individual can radically reject his class 'identity' and that rejection can inform his political and cultural prejudices. Nonetheless, caste and class are widely recognised as points of reference by individuals because they are linked to family, local community and recognisable traditions. Politically correct categories, by contrast, are more abstract and exist largely in the minds of a small band of activists. Anti-racist campaigners, who are more likely to be white than black, speak as if there were a single 'black' culture based on victimhood and resistance to 'white' oppression. Rarely, if ever, do they acknowledge that there is a wide variety of black cultures and within them individuals with a wide variety of attitudes towards politics and race. The idea that race defines political outlook is itself a form of racial prejudice, but this irony is lost on zealous campaigners, as they lump all 'black' people together and arbitrarily define their interests.

This process of 'lumping together' is central to politically correct classification. Ostensibly, it is a form of coalition building, sometimes referred to as 'rainbow' politics. The idea, adapted from the far left, is that a united front against the 'majority culture'[21], by diverse individuals and groups, will secure lasting social change. In reality, rainbow politics increases the power and voice of unrepresentative activists. At the same time, it takes power away from those on whose behalf activist groupings claim to speak, denying them a voice as individuals, riding roughshod over their experiences and values. Amongst black people in Britain, whether of African or Caribbean origins, there is a wealth of religious and spiritual cultures, predominantly Christian, but also Islamic and traditional African. Black churches play a more important role in the lives of many black people than race relations bureaucrats. Their role is seldom acknowledged by 'anti-racists', except to condemn them for 'sexism' or 'homophobia'. The underlying weakness of rainbow politics is exposed by such criticisms. For an alliance between 'anti-racist' activists, feminist ideologues and gay militants is at best artificial, given the social conservatism that prevails amongst Britain's black populations.[22] It is also wide of the mark, because of the widespread concern about family breakdown in black communities and the consequent wish to bolster familial stability. Black parents, concerned about bad schooling, have been in the forefront of efforts to restore traditional classroom teaching and oppose the false version of 'progressive' education imposed on their children.[23]

We have seen already the scorn that feminists can heap upon socially conservative women. This extends beyond women with strong religious beliefs to all women who disagree with feminism and reject the idea of a struggle between the sexes. The claim by 'women's groups' to speak for women is therefore specious in the extreme, whilst the idea that half of the population can be lumped together into an interest group would be ridiculous if it were not sinister and totalitarian. Yet the most inappropriate lumping together of all is that of male and female homosexuals. Both metaphorically and literally, they are strange bedfellows. In practice, there is no natural empathy between them, little, indeed, besides incomprehension and mutual hostility, because they live – and love - in entirely different ways. The activist myth, nonetheless, is that 'lesbians and gay men' (almost always in that order, to be politically correct) possess a common culture of oppression and share an 'enemy' in 'straight society'. In practice, lesbians of feminist disposition are over-represented in 'gay rights' movements, with men deferring meekly towards them, in a parodic reversal of the 'gender stereotypes' they denounce. Male homosexual radicals, who claim to be fighting for freedom and individual autonomy, display a remarkable readiness to act as useful idiots for a feminist ideology that is intrinsically antipathetic towards them as men. The confused assertions of David Fernbach, a founder of 'Gay Liberation', express well this confusion:

> [*After 1971*] relations between the lesbian and gay men's movements have shown a fairly typical pattern. First, there are specific lesbian organisations and groups, which exclude men exactly as does the women's movement in general. Second, there are groups that define themselves as 'gay', and are open to both women and men, though invariably with women finding themselves a minority. … The fact that lesbians can choose whether or not to work with men means that relations in mixed groups are generally harmonious. Where specifically male groups exist, it is usually to avoid the problem of tokenism; an example would be [*the*

long-since defunct] **Gay Left** magazine. In general, cooperation between lesbians and gay men is at a premium in civil rights struggles, particularly concerning discrimination at work or in housing, and in these cases joint action is very common. In counselling, consciousness raising, theoretical development, and struggles for social facilities, on the other hand, separatism is rather more general. Naturally, this question is always interpreted through a whole range of ideological perspectives.[24]

The skewed morality of political correctness is readily apparent in Fernbach's essay. It is taken as an article of faith that women 'can choose whether or not to work with men'. If men 'choose not to work with women', however, an ideologically pure reason such as 'avoiding tokenism' must be invented to justify that choice. In the 'mixed' groups Fernbach describes, women 'find themselves in a minority' for a very obvious reason: male homosexuality has, for whatever reason, always been more frequent than lesbianism. Ideology blinds him to facts about ordinary life that are clear to most people. One of these is that homosexual men enjoy male company and tend to flourish in all-male groups or occupations. This remains the case even if, as in the military or the Church, acceptance has meant concealing their sexual nature. Some, indeed, feel far more at home with heterosexual men than with most fellow-homosexuals. They are therefore quite uninterested in gay 'identity politics' and still less interested in forming coalitions with lesbians. On the contrary, it is to heterosexual women that they tend to be drawn as friends.

Since the time of Fernbach's piece, the rainbow coalition of sexual identity has reached new heights of absurdity with the inclusion of 'bisexuals' (of both sexes) and 'transgendered people'. Not surprisingly, this intensifies the anti-male bias of the 'gay rights' movement. Gay activists often accuse politically inactive or closeted homosexuals of 'self-hatred'.[25] However self-hatred is the very basis of the movement they have created. It is expressed through hatred for themselves as men and a corresponding denial that homosexuality is principally a male phenomenon and is connected to broader questions of masculinity. The result of such self-hatred and denial is a political movement out of step and incapable of communicating with those for whom it claims to speak.

The experience of homosexuals is replicated across the spectrum of 'identity politics'. The women's movement does not, as its exponents claim, belong to all women, because it is biased against those it considers to be 'traditional' or subservient to men. Most women love men, whether as husbands and fathers, sons or close personal friends. Feminist politics confuses affection and loyalty with subservience and so creates an emotionally arid climate for both sexes. Many feminists, especially those whom Christina Hoff Sommers designates 'gender feminists', regard androgyny as the ideal state. As a political and social aspiration, this is as inimical to most women as it is to most men and calls into question feminist support for genuine women's rights.

Feminists, it might be argued, tend to support the rights of idealised women, rather than champion women as they are.[26] Similarly, 'anti-racists' tend not to be interested in black cultures as they are. In many cases, they aim to impose on black people the values of 'enlightened' whites. With an uncanny resemblance to the missionaries and their converts in colonial times, they seek salvation for 'their' people in secular, Euro-centric ideologies. Until the early 1990s, Marxism predominated amongst these ideological 'systems'. Since then, it has given ground to free-market fundamentalism, 'universal human rights', feminism and the political correctness of 'liberal elites' in Western cities. These ideologies have in common a belief in 'progress' for its own sake, extreme materialism and contempt for traditional cultures. Chancellor Williams, an African-American, describes the phenomenon of black liberal self-hatred in terms as relevant to Europe and Africa as they are to the United States:

> The black people of the world have come at last to destiny's crossroads. … But there is a terrible crisis of leadership at the crossroads. There is no united leadership group or any real effort to create one. The great difficulty is that black leaders, unlike the Jews, do not know their own heritage. They are almost wholly ignorant of their own cultural source from which independent, original thinking springs and progress is inspired. The 'Negro' leaders who spearhead and carry on the campaigns for integration, not only do not know the heritage of the Blacks, they do not want to know it. They wish to draw on the Caucasian heritage …; they keep on trying, because the white 'liberals' do encourage them to hope by mixing with them from time to time. Other leaders, equally ignorant of their heritage, simply do not know which way to lead. They, too, feel compelled to adopt and follow Caucasian ideologies because they do not feel free, equal and competent enough to develop an ideology of their own, an African oriented ideology.[27]

Williams is, perhaps, simplistic in his belief that there is a unified 'black people of the world' who have a common interest. In this sense, he falls into the same trap as the white 'liberals' and their black allies, to whose attitudes he is opposed. His diagnosis of the pseudo-liberal ideology of race relations is, nonetheless, highly astute. For the anti-racist movement highlights difference at one level, and yet imposes universalist definitions of correct political and social behaviour. More seriously, the ideology of anti-racism is reductionist, identifying discrimination by white racists as the source of all evil, rather than as one problem among many, to be resolved where possible by consensual methods. This means that problems such as family disintegration, aesthetic and environmental deprivation and insecure employment are downplayed or overlooked. These are problems that many black people share with working-class whites and so should provide common ground. Raised by anti-racists as much as by their fascistic opponents, the issue of race stands in the way of constructive dialogue and the solving of shared social problems. Anti-racists claim that they believe in common citizenship. In practice they stand in the way of the development of racial harmony, whilst displaying a missionary-like intolerance towards minority cultures when they deviate from politically correct norms.

4. The New Stereotypes

One of the most oft-repeated shibboleths of identity politics is that it is about challenging stereotypes. Yet the very act of focusing on racial or sexual identity encourages people to think of others as 'different' or hostile, rather than as fellow citizens, or fellow-human beings. At the same time, it encourages individuals to identify characteristics that make them 'different' or 'disadvantaged' and then forge group identities based on resentment or hate. As always with forked tongued politics, some identities are more equal than others. 'Gay Pride' is liberating, whereas 'White Pride' would be a racist outrage. This is despite the growing evidence that the white working class have at least as much reason as homosexuals to feel discontent. They are, so to speak, the colour missing from the rainbow of 'diversity', abandoned by the left, despised by the 'liberal' centre and ignored by the moderate right.

Far right identity politics mirrors absolutely the politically correct campaigns. The British National Party's best-known slogan, 'Rights for Whites' echoes the slogans of 'gay rights' or 'a woman's right to choose [abortion]'.[1] Thus, the far right does an unwitting service to those who genuinely believe in freedom. It exposes the absurdity and bad faith underlying political correctness. For if we assume, as authoritarian liberals do, that gay pressure groups speak on behalf of *all* homosexuals, then we must assume that neo-fascists represent *all* whites. This is patent nonsense, as even the most hardened (and racially biased) anti-racist campaigner will have to admit.

If anything, identity politics perpetuates traditional stereotypes instead of calling them into question. Women, after all, are portrayed as vulnerable victims of 'patriarchy', in need of special protection by the state. Black people, similarly, are categorised as underprivileged. Politically, the black man is classed by the colour of skin and not the content of his character – by self-styled 'liberals' as well as by racists. 'Gay Pride' festivals – and the political agitation accompanying them – contribute to popular prejudices that homosexual men are effeminate and histrionic. The equation of male homosexual interests with those of lesbians and transsexuals curiously resembles the moralistic lumping together of the 'perversions' by pre-Freudian psychiatry. In addition to reinforcing old stereotypes, political correctness invents new ones. Instead of merely opening professions to women, the emphasis of feminism is on obliging women to have careers and making invisible those who choose not to do so. This is accompanied by a forked-tongued disdain for 'male roles' – unless women decide they wish to assume them. Identity politics is ambivalent about difference. It is founded on the appeal to Otherness, and yet claims to be breaking down barriers. It calls for an 'inclusive society', and yet regards mere integration as inadequate. Campaigners for identity-based movements use the rhetoric of equality before the law. At the same time, they argue that 'women' and 'minorities' should have special privileges and possess special insights. Nonetheless, they rarely seem to 'like' the people they represent. Much as the National Socialists berated constantly the German *Volk*, politically correct activists show little besides impatience and anger towards 'their' constituents when forced to treat them as individuals rather than mere group members. We have already seen that the ideology of gay liberation induces self-hatred in homosexual men, so that they submit voluntarily to anti-male activists. Here, David Fernbach shows his ideological dislike for fellow-homosexuals, as well as, more generally, his fellow men:

> The bad situation is compounded, in the gay male community especially, by the vicious effects of commercialism, by the way that society defines us in terms of our sexuality, and by our relative isolation from ties of family and community. In North America, where all these tendencies are far more developed than in Britain, the gay ghettos of the big cities display a lifestyle that centres on a numbing promiscuity, on the cult of the butch, macho image (indeed only an image, by which effeminate gay men seek to mystify both themselves and prospective sexual partners), on the spread of sadomasochism and other extreme forms of role-playing, and on the constant use of intoxicants such as amyl nitrate to enhance an otherwise jaded sexual palate. In Britain, the trend is in the same direction, though unlikely ever to develop to quite

the same degree. As always with such negative phenomena displayed by oppressed groups, from the traditional miserliness and fawning of the Jews through to the football hooliganism of working-class kids today, it is the situation of oppression that must be blamed, not something 'innate' about Jews, working-class youths, gays or whatever.[2]

Much of this propaganda could very easily have been written by a right-wing critic of homosexuality, a Christian fundamentalist or a prejudiced tabloid commentator. Were it written by a heterosexual, it would be vigorously denounced as 'homophobic'. Fernbach's approach also has uncanny echoes of the 'ex-gay' movement, a variant on the theme of identity politics, by which homosexual men convert to evangelical Protestantism, for the most part, announce that they have been 'cured' and denounce their previous 'sinful lifestyle'.[3] It might only be a matter of time before pro-feminist men proclaim themselves 'ex-males'. Like Christian evangelicals, politically correct campaigners believe that they have a duty to save mankind, beginning with the 'oppressed groups' they alternately elevate and despise.

The decline of socialism, and left-wing economics more generally, has assisted the rise of political correctness. Policies that were until very recently associated with the 'loony left' and so the butt of dry humour, have now become intellectual orthodoxies. Identity politics has assumed increasing prominence in public debate, at the same time as any other left-wing world-view is struggling for recognition. At a time when the very idea of public ownership and public service is under attack, the nationalised race and sex discrimination bureaucracies expand and acquire new powers. There are several reasons for this phenomenon. First, it is likely that identity politics attracts those who would once have been drawn towards the Far Left, with its blend of authoritarianism and rebelliousness. Secondly, the intellectual paralysis of liberalism has deprived those who believe in freedom of adequate political vocabulary to defend it. The belief in freedom for individuals, as opposed to rights for groups, is reduced to a series of popular instincts, excluded from a political culture that increasingly denies choice.

Third, it is no coincidence that political correctness and free-market fundamentalism have become orthodoxies at the same time. Both are based on a deterministic belief in 'progress', both seek wholly materialistic solutions to human problems, both are 'internationalist' in the sense that they have no respect for local customs or differences between nations. Both claim to promote 'diversity', but in practice seek to impose 'one-size-fits-all' solutions to economic and social problems. Both philosophies contend that human beings are essentially plastic, that constants in human nature can be legislated away or abolished by the play of market forces. Identity politics inherits from Marxism the idea of groups engaged in economic struggle with each other. It shares with free market fundamentalism the belief that there is no such thing as a civil society with a common purpose, merely a plethora of competing individuals and groups. Identity politics and free-market fundamentalism hold in common a shallow view of the individual, interpreting his or her well-being entirely in terms of material advancement. This encourages him to retreat from civil society, to become a consumer of, rather than a participant in the political process – a consumer of identity-based 'rights' much as he is a consumer of brand products.

The abstract rights for which identity movements strive so assiduously are presented as if they were commodities, for material gratification, aimed at niche markets. Unlike the rights endowed by the Creator in the American Declaration of Independence, politically correct 'rights' are collective before they are individual and deny any spiritual origin or point of reference. In this sense, the rhetoric of group rights resembles closely the 'economic and social rights' of the former Soviet Union and present-day China. One recent paean to human rights legislation in Britain is entitled 'Values for a Godless Age'. This is a highly tendentious claim that raises abstract 'rights' to the level of a secular religion.[4] Its arrogance calls to mind the attempt by French Revolutionaries to enforce the worship of abstract Reason. This cult, the political correctness of its day, accompanied a period of Terror that reduced the Declaration of the Rights of Man to a surreal work of fiction.

In the context of British politics, the parallel rise of identity-based movements and market fundamentalism coincides with the breakdown of the post-war political and economic consensus, based on the mixed economy and the welfare state. That consensus might have been bureaucratic in many ways and often inclined towards collectivism. Yet for the most part, it had until the late 1970s reflected the benign characteristics of British political life. Chief amongst these were the concept of individual freedom under the rule of law, freedom of speech and expression, social responsibility and tolerance, at both individual and communal levels. In so far as these characteristics prevailed, British political culture could be described as civilised. With their erosion, some countervailing negative influences were reasserted. These included class hatred, narrow or selfish economic individualism, ideological rigidity and an authoritarian approach to moral – and especially sexual – questions.

Ideological rigidity is more characteristic of British politics than is widely appreciated, partly because of some inherently adversarial elements in the political system.[5] In the late 1970s, it was resurgent on left and right. Moral authoritarianism, by then, went far beyond traditional disapproval of cohabitation, homosexuality or sexually explicit literature, although pro-censorship campaigns were being successfully revived. However a new strain of left-wing moralism had also arisen. Orthodox Communism, historically weak in Britain, was (from Stalin's time especially) conservative on moral and sexual matters, one reason why it was scorned by the New Left. British socialism, which is said to owe more to Methodism than Marx, has a strong puritanical undertone.

The 'Nonconformist Conscience', to which Oscar Wilde once famously fell victim, has been strongly represented in both Labour and Liberal politics. New Left moralism, by contrast, presents the Nonconformist Conscience in reverse. Instead of regarding legal abortion as a necessary evil, or rather the lesser of two evils in some circumstances[6], New Left moralists extol as a social virtue the woman's 'right to choose'. Opponents or even mild critics of this position are vilified with a zeal worthy of religious bigots of the most puritanical stripe. In general, New Left moralists reverse the puritan ethos of the Nonconformist denominations. This means that restraint becomes a sin and sexuality a political 'right' instead of a gift conferring responsibilities on individuals. The prejudice about homosexuality is inverted, so that 'homophobia' becomes a moral outrage. This ethic of tolerance extends, of course, only to homosexual men who read from the script of minority rights and co-operate with feminists. Racism is also a sin, but ethnic minorities who oppose the race industry are treated as outcasts.[7] The secular morality of the New Left, based on fanaticism combined with sentimentality, presents a closed ideological framework, like the brand of Marxism that challenged the liberal values of the academy:

There have always been ideologies, but our age is notable for the number and virulence of them: minor ones like Scientology; major ones like Nationalism, Racism, Feminism, Marxism. And of them all, Marxism is the most influential, well-organised and intelligent.

The trick in making an ideology is to manufacture a range of words (or re-define old ones by statement and repetition) so that a deliberate effort at persuasion and enlistment can be passed off as neutral description. And Marxism, as the pre-eminent ideology, has an arsenal of such terms: 'proletariat', 'class struggle', 'bourgeois', 'class consciousness', 'alienation', 'imperialism', etc. Independent thought is impossible when using these words; the answers are built in from the beginning.[8]

[*My emphasis*]

Although Marxist ideology has declined (but not disappeared), its methods persist in the group classifications of political correctness. New words and phrases, precluding reasoned argument or critical thought, have increased the activist lexicon. Chief amongst such shibboleths are: gender; racism; sexism; 'lesbian and gay'; homophobia; discrimination; 'Equal Opportunities'; inclusive language; diversity; positive action, and – with the most serious implications for genuine liberals – human rights. Most of these terms are, so to speak, indigenous to single-issue radicalism. Crucially, however, some have been expropriated from traditional liberalism. A notable example is human rights. Until recently, these denoted the rule of law, freedom of speech, association and thought, and the dignity of the individual above all. In the post-war era, they brought the promise of liberal values, applied flexibly, without dogma and with due regard for differences between cultures. The 'rights' themselves were balanced by responsibilities, whether political or economic. They were not ends in themselves, but part of the broader framework of a just (but still imperfect) society.

To a large extent, human rights still carry that connotation. However, the phrase is co-opted increasingly by identity politics campaigners, so that the distinction between 'human rights' for individuals and collective rights defined by unrepresentative pressure groups is harder for the conscientious liberal to discern. We may therefore see the decline of liberalism as a vicious circle. The weakness of liberal intellectuals in the face of an authoritarian-collectivist onslaught has been compounded by the hijacking of liberal terms of reference. The defection to the identity politics camp of liberal academics and policy makers (typified by the 'anti-admin' liberals at PNL) has been compounded by the equally damaging defection of many traditional liberals to right-wing conservatism (typified by the 'pro-admin liberals'). Meanwhile, the ascendancy of political correctness has been aided by the decline of socialism as a credible philosophy and the retreat of traditional liberals to their left and their right. This large-scale surrender has retarded the development of a rigorous liberal critique of identity politics. It has enabled an authoritarian, collectivist ideology to assume the liberal mantle, abuse liberal vocabulary and cynically manipulate liberal sensibilities for totalitarian ends.

*

Let us return, for a moment, to where we began the previous chapter, with my younger self as a schoolboy in the dentist's waiting room who laughed at the satirical cartoon. My interest in politics was also just beginning and the Britain in which I lived was on the cusp of economic and cultural change. The loosely social democratic order was unravelling around me, whilst authoritarian collectivism and 'market forces' dogma were simultaneously gathering momentum. For a schoolboy, unlike an adult, the personal and the political are genuinely and necessarily connected. Much of my laughter, therefore, probably arose from the reference to social workers. This is because a social worker and her husband had recently moved into the house next door. She was a kindly woman, liked by my parents and her other neighbours. It was clear, nonetheless, that she did not regard the children, poor people or prisoners with whom she worked as fully intelligent human beings, either in the sense of requiring discipline and purpose, or of having the freedom to think for themselves and make moral choices. Indeed I recall that she spoke of her clients less as individuals and more as lists of symptoms, rather like the type of doctor who refers to patients by the names of their diseases. She was not a lady with any great interest in ideas. Instead, quite appropriately, she believed in solving practical problems in practical ways, and set about this with great energy. For this I respected her. Underlying her practicality, however, was the unquestioned assumption that such solutions would be rational, secular, materialistic and administered almost wholly by the state. It was as if, rather than dealing with individual problems, she dealt with individuals as problems. And through this process, individuality was lost but the problems multiplied.

This distinction, between individual problems and individuals as problems, is important if we are to understand the shift in political language and practice over the last thirty years: a shift from individual freedom towards group rights. Such a shift was already underway in British political culture at the time of that cartoon of the Three 'Ethnic' Bears; it had already 'advanced' much further in the United States. From roughly the same time, I recall a comedy sketch on television, in which the Two Ronnies (Corbett and Barker) dressed up as char ladies and discussed a wide range of subjects, from the honours system ('will we have "Member of the Common Market" instead of MBE?') to changing popular attitudes towards black Britons. 'I used to like them', one of them said, 'until you had to'.

A sketch like this would not be shown on British television now, officially because it might 'offend some people', in reality because it expresses a truth unpalatable to today's opinion formers – that multiculturalism, when imposed by the state, creates hatred or distrust between races, but that true tolerance evolves without our being told what to think, say and do. I grew up in the 'golden age' of comedy, after the old, moralistic censorship had been abolished, but before the new politically correct censorship had been introduced. It was a time when male comics could be marvellously smutty, and at the same time dignified and articulate, whilst the comediennes could be feminine, elegant and kind-hearted as well as outrageous. Sadism and nihilism were largely absent from comedy, although they were well-represented in pop music and the 'alternative' press. Political satire was sharp and merciless, but non-partisan, attacking hypocrisy and cant from wherever it came. Camp innuendo was widespread, well-loved and wholly free of the self-righteous aggression of politicised homosexuality. All that is changed utterly now, reflecting less a change in the wider culture of what people think, believe and want, but more the success of an elite in imposing its ideas about change.

There is, admittedly, a spirit of nostalgia in some of these recollections. In remembering cartoon strips and comic sketches of the past, there is the temptation to retreat to a time before 'things went wrong' and thereby avoid trying to disentangle problems. That is a comfortable position, adopted by many cultural conservatives, but it is a position that accepts defeat and so will not do. In any case, the nostalgic sentiments are all highly qualified. I look back to that time of better comedy sketches, and more civilised political commentary, not as a true golden age, but as a time of transition, the start of a shift of emphasis in liberal thought away from the individual and towards the group, away from freedom as an ideal, towards the demand for 'rights', based on claims on behalf of one group to the detriment of another. This change has affected the way we talk and think about politics. It has altered profoundly intellectual discourse and, through a smoke ring effect, extended to many and varied areas of life, from journalism to social work, from our work to our leisure, from the office, factory or barracks through to private relationships and voluntary activities.

But it is for another reason that I recall the comedians' good-humoured sniping at the race relations lobby. For they reflected quite accurately a public mood that was as much sceptical and irreverent as it was conformist, that was rebellious as well as traditionalist, indi-vidualistic and tolerant as well as, at times, quite prejudiced and inward looking. In other words, a complex, constantly evolving culture, full of contradictions, where an individual could vigorously oppose immigration but at the same time regard his black colleagues as friends, where a woman could hate feminism but pursue a suc-cessful professional career, or where a homosexual could be content-ed with his orientation but profoundly hostile to the gay rights campaign. This is a culture of contradictions, where the lofty dilemmas of liberal thought – the balance between the individual and civil society, public and private, change and tradition – are played out on a case by case basis every day, sometimes with good will and humour, other times with irritation.

British society, like other Western-type societies, is based on this process of continuous, often untidy compromise. It is made up of individuals who, in most cases, are guided less by an overarching ideology than by a series of influences. These influences may be polit-ical or religious, but often they are not. They are rooted in experience, family background, economic circumstances, by varied allegiances, such as to region or profession, by interests, hobbies, difficult deci-sions or personal observations. Above all, they are *individual* influ-ences, part of the individual's character and hence impervious to ide-ological classifications.

In a free society, political institutions – and political discourse – should reflect such variations, if they are to function properly. They should encourage unfettered discussion, but at the same time point the way towards compromise, justice and tolerance. In so doing, they may be partisan but they should not attempt to impose on the population as a whole an official ideology. This is because justice, at individual and social levels, depends on the admission of human fallibility. There are few universal rules of politics, but one is that no system geared towards the perfectibility of man has provided either freedom or fulfilment for its citizens, still less economic prosperity. The liberal state is based on the idea that society is a constantly evolving organism. Such evolution is not a neat line of historically inevitable 'progress'. Like living organisms, societies may expand and contract, or even decay. They can be guided, but they cannot, anymore than individual men and women, be forced into neat, predictable patterns. The attempt to impose an official ideology is therefore ultimately incompatible with a free society, destroys the possibility of compromise and points towards totalitarian rule. As wrote the US Supreme Court Justice Robert Jackson, who presided over the Nuremberg trials:

> If there is any fixed star in our constitutional constellation, it is that no official, high or petty, can prescribe what shall be orthodox politics, nationalism, religion, or other matter.[9]

The liberal state is defined by its absence of an official ideology, a state-imposed dogma to which all citizens must make obeisance. Yet this does not imply an absence of values. Indeed the very reverse is true. The ideology is absent because a belief in the freedom and innate dignity of the individual underlie that society and its institutions. It is a freedom that is inborn, or expressed another way, endowed by the Creator, providing a stable background against which competing ideas are tested and absorbed. This process depends on a shared sense that continuity is important, and that it is achieved by the rule of law, and by structures such as the family and the local community, which lie outside the state's immediate remit. Far from preventing change, the sense of continuity permits constructive reform, and the persistence of shared values permits free expression, dissent and ridicule (often justified) of established authority and norms without descending into chaos. In the liberal state, the sense of continuity *absorbs* the demand for change, as both are essential ingredients of a free society. For, as Richard Clutterbuck, the soldier turned political scientist, puts it:

A rigid society can never be stable, nor can it be comfortable to live in. Vegetation under disused concrete will eventually break out. It will smash the concrete, but it will itself have endured a hard and frustrated existence before it does so. And a man is a good deal more dynamic than a vegetable.[10]

Without an official ideology, real change can be implemented coherently, new ideas explored, whilst protest, satire and personal eccentricity can be positively valued, as well as accepted as part of life. A society free of official dogmatism tends to be a more inventive society, more creative in the arts and sciences, more open to ideas that turn conventional assumptions on their heads. The ecology movement, for example, has since the late 1960s challenged the idea of economic growth as the key to human happiness and progress. In so doing, it has questioned the most basic assumptions of Western political and intellectual life since the industrial era began. This more holistic approach has influenced mainstream thought to the extent that Marxists reinvent themselves as 'red-greens', corporate board-rooms oversee 'environmental audits' and politicians of all established parties lean over backwards to assert their 'green' credentials.

There are times, therefore, when green politics looks dangerously close to becoming an official ideology, but it is saved from this by its diverse nature. The green spectrum encompasses Deep Ecologists, who acknowledge the connections between conservatism and conservation, green socialists or Social Ecologists, who blame capitalism for environmental degradation, and green capitalists who believe that ecological problems can be solved better by the unfettered market than the state. Green politics, at its best, provides a critique of the over-sized, impersonal state. It believes that restoring the connection between individual and government is as important as breaking down the artificial divide between 'Man' and 'Nature'. This is, in most respects, a restatement of Aristotle's wise counsel against expansionism, for he believed that there are natural limits to the size of states, 'just as there are limits to the size of plants and animals'. True ecologists, therefore, are not trying to destroy Western culture, but to restore its best principles of respect for the individual. At the same time, they intend to restore to economics its original meaning of 'good housekeeping':

We have seen that man in our present society has been deprived of a satisfactory social environment. A society made up of decentralised, self-sufficient communities, in which people work near their homes, have the responsibility of governing themselves, of running their own schools, hospitals and welfare services, in fact of running their own communities, should, we feel, be a much happier place. Its members, in these conditions, would be likely to develop an identity of their own, which many of us have lost in the mass society we live in. They would tend, once more, to find an aim in life, develop a set of values and take pride in their achievement as well as in those of their community.[11]

The example of green politics shows that new ideas evolve, and exercise influence, within the context of a free society, and that only within free – and ideologically unbiased – societies, can really effective and positive changes take place. On the surface, this proposition seems fairly obvious. It is, nonetheless, frequently forgotten by economists, political scientists and 'experts' of all kinds. For despite the misery wrought by totalitarian movements, and their utter failure to improve the lot of mankind, totalistic solutions are by no means out of fashion. Ironically, since the fall of the Berlin Wall, there is a greater 'choice' of authoritarian collectivist movements available to the consumer of ideologies. These include radical feminism, free-market fundamentalism, extreme distortions of religious teachings and a perverse new version of 'human rights' that takes as its starting point the aims of collective entities and not the wishes of individuals.

These ideological tendencies might seem to have little in common. However they are united in the belief that their presuppositions are universally applicable, admit of no exceptions – individual or cultural – and so must be universally imposed, by force where necessary. Their supporters share an irrational, even superstitious belief, that they have a direct line to human destiny, that history, progress or divine powers are on their side. Politics, they believe, is not a patchwork of losses and gains, but an instrument for refashioning human nature. And so despite the demise of the 'great' totalitarian movements of the twentieth century, the totalitarian impulse remains undimmed. The all-encompassing totalitarian ideologies of far left and far right still exist, but they have for the most part given way to lesser totalitarianisms, or rather to forms of extremism that take single issues as their starting point. Their intention is to transform society and irrevocably alter human behaviour, but the 'ultimate goal' is less coherent than that of previous ideologies. The watchwords of these single-issue, totalistic movements are change, equality and rights. Yet through their rhetoric and their practice, they point the way to a society where the right to criticise is curtailed or abolished, equality before the law gives way to special pleading, social evolution to authoritarian stasis.

Without free political institutions, real change becomes impossible. Intellectual stagnation reigns, in a process once likened by John Stuart Mill to foot binding in imperial China. This is because no official space is provided for ideas other than stale clichés and state orthodoxies. Hence there is little possibility of dissent or questioning of accepted practices, and so few opportunities for pragmatic reform. This is a principal reason why authoritarian regimes become ossified and why they tend, eventually, to collapse. They lack that facility for self-criticism, which is often the key to political survival.

There is, therefore, an explicit connection between political freedom and constructive, lasting change. The eradication of poverty through universal welfare provision is one of the avowed goals of totalitarian movements, especially (but not exclusively) those of the left.[14] However the most successful welfare reforms have come about in conditions of democratic stability rather than revolution. In the European context, for example, the most successful welfare provision has developed in the most stable, cohesive nation-states, where change has been selective, incremental and based on consent. This brings us to the superficially less obvious link, between tradition and change, which collectivist ideologies ignore. Tradition and change balance each other: they are the Yin and the Yang of good politics. Lasting changes, such as social justice and ecological awareness are based on adapting and building upon traditional institutions rather than attempting to tear them down. This is why regimes derived from ideological contempt for the past fail so markedly to improve future prospects.

Successful reform, therefore, depends on political freedom and on a concept of civil society wider than that of the new liberals. Successful change, meanwhile, depends on regard for tradition, for these apparently contradictory principles in fact reinforce each other. By the same token, freedom itself depends on restraint – restraint voluntarily exercised because of an ethical code. Tolerance similarly depends on strong, shared principles of right and wrong, or more controversially 'normal' and 'abnormal'. Such shared values include respect for the individual, belief in freedom of speech and thought and social responsibility. The latter quality enables the individual to acknowledge that freedom survives through voluntary restraint. Or rather, he sees his freedom as a gift or a privilege instead of an unrestrained right, a resource to be carefully managed, rather than squandered. That is what Burke meant when he contrasted the 'manly, moral regulated liberty' he saw in British political culture with the blood-soaked abstractions of the French Revolution. It is what Clutterbuck describes here, as part of his analysis of the 'New Left' and the motives behind its championing of 'permissiveness'. It is worth remembering that many former members of that New Left are today the movers and shakers of British, American and continental European politics:

> The real target for attack is the public's confidence and belief in its way of life. All communities, from the most primitive to the most civilised, have evolved a system of laws and morals designed to preserve the serenity of their lives and the propagation of healthy offspring. Thus most tribal and most sophisticated societies have in some way tried to check the dissipation of sexual instincts into directions other than the production of children within some kind of stable family circle which can sustain and protect them until they reach maturity. The human animal is unique in requiring some sixteen years for this process, when the adolescent has developed the strength, dexterity and mental skills to survive independently. … The natural instinct for 'pair-bonding' in humans [lasts] for far longer than other animals. To supplement and fortify such instincts, tribal societies introduced taboos, and most civilizations have deterred homosexuality and other deviations, punished adulterers, discouraged promiscuity, encouraged monogamy (or at least restricted polygamy as in Islam) and have done much to foster stable family structures (nuclear or extended) in which children can grow up. Widely diverse communities in different parts of the world, without contact with each other, have independently evolved fairly similar restraints and customs for these purposes.
>
> The legal enforcement of these restraints and customs has, with those for the defence of life and property, been the main concern of the 'governments' which communities have accepted for their collective organisation throughout recorded history. It is for this reason that they are selected as particular targets by those who wish to erode or destroy existing forms of society.[12]

What we now call political correctness is the chaos of the 'permissive society' congealed into an authoritarian dogma. Whilst claiming to be the harbinger of freedom and diversity, this dogma increases the power of the state, and big business, over the individual. It does so by eroding the intermediary structures of civil society: the family; the local community; voluntary associations (except for those that serve political agendas); and the ethos of self-restraint. Far from encouraging diversity, the partisans of politically correctness try to enforce one-size-fits-all solutions. These ignore differences between individuals and assume that the human species can be moulded by 'enlightened' legislation or brainwashing.

Politically correct dogma, therefore, provides for ineffably bad government. Good government is that which works with, rather than against, the grain of human nature. It is about taking human beings as they are, rather than what small groups of activists would have them be. It is, in general, non-ideological, although it may be guided by ethical principles, both religious and secular. The aim of good government is fairness for all individuals, rather than 'equality' between groups. Good government recognises that man is territorial by nature and so does not attempt to impose artificial, multinational states, governed by bureaucrats who scorn the desire for independence. It realises also that there are positive and worthwhile differences between men and women, and so does not force them to adopt the same roles. The arbitrary injustice dispensed by politically correct campaigners is becoming apparent, to their supposed beneficiaries as much as their natural opponents. This offers the prospect of a rejection of group rights in favour of individual freedom within civil society: true liberalism, in place of the politics of the forked tongue.

5. Liberalism and Pseudo-Liberalism

In 1950, Theodor Adorno and his colleagues of the post-Marxist Frankfurt School produced *The Authoritarian Personality*. This was a two-volume study of the 'prejudiced person' and the psycho-political origins of the radical right. A subtle work and although flawed in some important respects and very much a product of its time, it remains a seminal study of authoritarian, right-wing impulses. For a critical distinction is drawn between the genuine conservative, who is a traditionalist, a patriot and an individualist, and the pseudo-conservative, whose attitudes are reactionary, collectivist and ethnocentric.[1]

Pseudo-conservatism was defined by the authors as a pathological undercurrent of politics, a mutation from true conservatism, influenced by collectivist, authoritarian modes of thought of left as well as right-wing origins. Fascism, for example, grew as much out of the anarcho-syndicalist tradition as conservative nationalist thought, whilst the 'socialism' in National Socialism was taken seriously by a significant wing of the Nazi party. Both fascism and Nazism are identified as pseudo-conservative political movements, brought from the fringe to the centre of power by the breakdown of shared values, extreme economic instability and the trauma of the Great War. These pathological forms of politics will triumph when economic and social conditions themselves become pathological. They are akin to collective hysteria in times of spiritual crisis, or to the disturbed behaviour of children when their family lives are in disarray.

Movements of the extreme right appeal to traditionalist impulses which cross economic and social boundaries. They lament the loss of continuity in politics, the breakdown of hierarchy, the loss of familiar patterns of behaviour. They seek the support of those who fear change and wish to resist it, yet their aim is neither to restore nor conserve. Such movements are 'pseudo-conservative' precisely because their true intentions are radical, but they disguise their radicalism with slogans aimed at natural conservatives. In practice, their targets are almost identical to those of the Left: traditional authority, hierarchy, political moderation, freedom of association, speech and thought, and objective intellectual inquiry. They are opposed to 'elitism', whether social or intellectual, associate political compromise with weakness and treachery, but wish to substitute for the old elite a new one, which can interpret the will of the people and enforce it. Right-wing radicals espouse a superficially strident nationalism, but they reject the idea of the nation as an entity that has evolved over centuries and substitute for it a myth of nationhood, transcending the historical nation, which is flawed, weakened and unreformable, appealing instead to a mythical Golden Age. This partially explains why the transition from anarchism to fascism has been so easy for some political activists. For the anarchist dismisses most of human history as worthless because it is based on authority and the state. His aim is to return, without sacrificing modern technology, to an egalitarian primitivism, usually associated (on sketchy archaeological evidence) with Neolithic Man, but sometimes falsely identified with today's tribal peoples.

The anarchist and the fascist both idealise the tribe. To the former, it is a society of equals, free of hierarchy and dominance. To the latter, it is a primitive warrior band based on blood ties, and unlike more 'civilised' warrior cultures, free from moral restraint. Both are quite uninterested in the reality of tribal societies, ancient or modern, or at least in any reality that conflicts with their prejudices. Indeed they regard myth as more important than history, and intuition as more important than reason. Here they differ from the orthodox Marxist. Although he tends to be dogmatic and inflexible, the Marxist believes in both reason and history. His analysis of society might be based on conflict and might lead him to profoundly illiberal conclusions, such as sweeping antipathy to tradition, contempt for spiritual values and the belief that the individual should be told what is good for him. He is, in Karl Popper's terms, 'historicist' in his outlook, because he believes that history is following an inexorable course, which the politically conscious are able to discern. Yet much of Marxist political discussion is about interpreting history, or analysing current events in an historical light.

Fascists and anarchists, by contrast, dismiss history in favour of myth and reasoned analysis in favour of 'feeling' or intuition. This characteristic they share with feminists, who dismiss history as 'patri-archal' and reason as masculine. In their game of linguistic distor-tion, they substitute a mythological 'herstory', in which a Golden Age of matriarchy and goddess worship plays a dominant role. Like anar-chists, they idealise the Neolithic age, which they interpret as a time of pre-historic peace and reverence for nature, spoiled by the myste-rious development of agriculture, property and 'male domination'.[2] Like fascists, they revere the tribe, which they regard as egalitarian, collectivist and lacking distinctions between public and private spheres. All the single-issue movements that comprise the new liber-alism place myth above history and emotion above reason. Multiculturalists, for instance, pretend that all of the Ancient Egyptians were 'black', ignoring quite clear evidence to the contrary. Propagandists for gay rights assert that the Ancient Greeks 'accepted homosexuality', ignoring both cultural differences within Greece and the complex rules that governed erotic relationships between men. To such campaigners, historical truth is less relevant than group 'self-esteem', a concept, incidentally, that is also beloved of the extreme right, which elevates racial or national 'self-esteem' above all other considerations, in particular freedom and tolerance.

As well as being pseudo-conservative, the extreme right as Adorno defines it is *pseudo-nationalist*, or more precisely supra-nationalist. Racial nationalism, after all, transcends political frontiers when it invokes ethnic identity. It subordinates, to an ideal of racial unity, such differences as language, religion, political development and law. Such differences are signs of weakness and failure, rather than welcome variations. A hallmark of fascism in Europe has been a wish to dissolve the nation state and replace it with an ideal type of nation, based on racial affinity, with a uniform culture and a stan-dardised political system. Significantly, the first political party after World War II to call openly for a pan-European state without borders was Sir Oswald Mosley' s Union Movement, successor to the British Union of Fascists. A pan-European state was one of the original aims of the Europe's far right. Its language finds ironic echo today in that of self-styled progressives favouring European integration, or in their terms an 'ever-closer union' between 'Europe's peoples'.[3]

In spite of its pseudo-conservatism, the extreme right believes in 'progress' and regards the motive force of politics as continuous change. Unlike the left (with the possible exception of Trotskyists), its appeal is to unreason and sentimentality, rather than reasoned analysis of society. The repudiation of reason and the elevation of sentiment are characteristics of the new liberalism, too, as are supra-nationalism, contempt for historical accuracy and dislike for 'elitist' tradition. Like the fascist movements of the past, and their imitators today, new liberalism takes as its starting point the group instead of the individual. The group is supra-national, although it might well be derived from race. Group membership becomes a neo-tribal loyalty that overrides moral constraints and custom, accumulated wisdom and even compliance with the law. It combines the anarchist myth of 'equality' with a fascistic will to power, the power of one or more groups over others. There is, in the action and behaviour of new liberals, little concept of political democracy, or of individual freedom under the rule of law. Instead, the democratic political system is viewed as a hostile force, an enemy to be captured, manip-ulated and subdued until it gives way to a spoils system, whereby power is distributed between interest groups favoured by race and sex, or rather those self-appointed representatives of 'women and minorities'. The group, for new liberals, fulfils the same function as 'race and nation' for the extreme right.

Thus the new liberalism's resemblance to fascist ideology is more marked than its resemblance to the left. Half a century after Adorno, therefore, it is fitting that we should draw upon his analysis of the right when we consider recent changes in liberal thought. This is not because the right-wing bogeyman has disappeared. Rather, it is because the liberal-left bogeyperson has arrived and manages at once to threaten individual liberty and undermine liberalism as a credible political ideal. To understand what has happened to liberal politics, it is helpful to draw a second distinction: between 'true liberals' and 'pseudo-liberals', as well as liberalism old and new. The true liberal believes in individual freedom under the rule of law, the removal of obstacles to individual success and a society which aims to be tolerant and fair-minded. He accepts that freedom depends for its survival on respect between individuals who disagree with each other, and on a culture that encourages polite behaviour, rational argument, good manners and voluntary restraint. The true liberal recognises as well that certain areas of private life, and certain public institutions, possess distinctive and valuable cultures on which external change should not be imposed. Thus he will oppose any moves to impose 'anti-discrimination' laws on places of worship or private clubs, because the principles of freedom of religion, and freedom of association, override the doctrine of equality. He will also oppose attempts to compel the Armed Forces to accommodate politically correct demands that conflict with their ethos and traditions. This is because the true liberal will recognise that operational effectiveness and unit cohesion come before the dogma of 'Equal Opportunities'. Unlike the ideologue of right or left, he accepts that reforms should be incremental, that positive traditions should be preserved, that there are constants in human nature that reformers ignore at their peril. In short, he believes that treating people fairly does not mean forcing them to be 'equal', and that the general principle of opportunity does not require interference in private realms, nor forcing inappropriate change on institutions that work well. For if liberal principles become inflexible and coercive, then they both lose their value as principles and cease to be liberal at all.

The pseudo-liberal, by contrast, demands a socially engineered 'equality'. This concept has little, if anything, to do with fairness. To most pseudo-liberals, extreme disparities of income are of little concern, unless they are differences in pay between men and women or differences between one 'ethnic group' and another. One of the mantras of pseudo-liberalism is 'commitment to Equal Opportunities'. Unlike genuine equality of opportunity, a goal once shared by socialists, liberals and many conservatives, 'Equal Opportunities' are not about individuals but groups. This means that under the pretext of 'anti-discrimination', discriminatory devices are zealously revived. In the early 1960s, for example, college application forms in the United States '*included a blank line on which all prospective students were required to indicate their race*'.[4] Such indications were used to discriminate against black and other 'non-white' applicants. At the behest of the civil rights movement, these questionnaires were abolished. Now, on both sides of the Atlantic, they are one of the principal rites of 'Equal Opportunities'. They are used in application forms for almost all public, and many private, appointments and are an increasing feature of consumer surveys.[5] Their intention is to classify the population along racial or ethnic lines, and hence to discriminate 'positively' in favour of certain groups and – with the inclusion of sex as well as race – to enshrine discrimination against men.

Thus, in the name of abstract equality, the principle of equality before the law is denied to large numbers of individuals. Employment, be it public or private, is viewed as an opportunity for social engineering, and as a further mechanism for distributing power between groups. To pseudo-liberals, the idea of opportunity for individuals of whatever background gives way to the politics of preference.

Sometimes that preference is racial, but most frequently it is the furtherance of feminist goals: the building of middle-class female careers disguised as opportunity for all.[6] Of late, and with encouragement from European Union bureaucrats[7], the true aim of 'Equal Opportunities' policies is stated more openly in Britain. 'Applications from women and ethnic minorities especially welcome' is the post-modern version of 'No Irish Need Apply'. But unlike 'No Irish Need Apply' signs, which were the work of privately unenlightened individuals, reverse discrimination is endorsed by a British state that follows a policy of divide-and-rule. It is promoted actively by those pan-European institutions that seek to supplant the nation state, although they lack true democratic legitimacy and have no true political roots.

In contrast to true equality of opportunity, a liberal principle directed at individuals, 'Equal Opportunities' programmes are aimed at groups, and so depend on the idea that society is irrevocably divided into groups and that these groups compete perpetually for new 'rights'. They are about tokenism rather than fair treatment, symbolic gestures rather than attempts to address profound and underlying social problems, such as poverty in the midst of plenty. Crucially, 'Equal Opportunities' are a device to confer power and special privileges on self-declared representatives of groups, at the expense of social cohesion and instead of helping our most disadvantaged citizens, whatever their race, and whether they happen to be female or male. For the pseudo-liberal detests the idea of a cohesive society, based on shared values. A strong civil society de-politicises the population, in that it makes political intervention in most areas of life at once unnecessary and undesired. It reduces the appeal of political activism. It limits the power of the state over the individual and the community he inhabits. Pseudo-liberalism is ultimately *about* power and so its adherents prefer to balkanise society into factions, jostling with each other for political space, fighting for special privileges, destroying trust between citizens and bullying those they purport to represent.

In this sphere, as in so many others, the pseudo-liberal speaks with forked tongue. Loudly he proclaims his hatred of competition, his preference for co-operative endeavour and his desire to rid society of aggressive impulses, which are invariably male in origin. Much of 'progressive' educational theory is based on the idea that aggression can be abolished, rather than channelled in positive directions, such as independence of mind or the ability to think and argue. To the pseudo-liberal ideologue, it matters little that his desire to stamp out natural aggression requires coercion and browbeating on a grand scale. Or, indeed, that his own ideology is aggressive, intrusive and intolerant. However one does not need to delve too far to discover the pseudo-liberal's true attitude to competition. He dislikes honest contests between individuals and shies away from open intellectual debate. At the same time, he promotes under the banner of 'Equal Opportunities' an eternally competitive struggle. Equality is transformed into a secular grail, the quest for which involves group conflict, rather than co-operation between citizens, group slogans in place of independent thought.

To pseudo-liberals, equality is therefore a mystical, irrational ideal, beyond definition and hence impossible to achieve. Thus elevated in theory, its pursuit is reduced politically to a war of all against all. This is not the anarchic individualism of Hobbes's State of Nature, the war of 'every man against every man'. Rather, it is a modernised form of tribal warfare, with sex and sexual orientation as substitute tribes, as well as old-fashioned 'race'. As in similar forms of warfare, there is no area of politics, or life, exempt from conflict. And so the workplace, the home, the school and the academy, Parliament, the law, the Armed Forces and the free press all lose their inherent value, as staples of a liberal society. Their distinctive histories, their ethos and their contributions to national life have no signiciance at all, except where they are useful objects of derision or convenient targets for egalitarian levelling-down. For to the pseudo-liberal mentality, they have ceased to be legitimate institutions in their own right. Instead, they are pawns in a larger political campaign, as relentless as it is lacking in conscience, as vocal as it is lacking in nobility.

Thus the pseudo-liberal vision of equality differs markedly from the liberal goal of a just society. The former, rigid and doctrinaire, is to be imposed by force. The latter, piecemeal and pragmatic, is to be introduced gradually and by consent. The former admits of no exceptions to its 'Equal Opportunities' edicts, the latter accepts that there are differences between individuals and respects distinctive institutions, including those whose values are not egalitarian at all. For the true liberal, forcing all individuals and all institutions to adopt the same values is authoritarian, even fascistic. It is incompatible with freedom and hence contradicts all notions of fairness, all principles of good politics. Pseudo-liberal *equality*, then, is quite different from liberal *equity*. Its relationship to Marxist egalitarianism is more ambivalent, indeed more forked-tongued. When the Marxist defines equality in terms of the classless society, he is expressing an ideal which, like 'Equal Opportunities', is absolutist in theory and impossible in practice. Attempts to realise both ideals result in extensive state coercion, grave injustice and the devaluing of the individual.

Class for the Marxist, like race or sex for the pseudo-liberal, is about collective loyalty. Nonetheless, the Marxist theory of class struggle is based ultimately on economics. The achievement of a classless society is based on a change in economic relationships, that is to say the abolition of private ownership and its replacement by common ownership. Pseudo-liberalism, by contrast, is weak and fatalistic on economics. The pseudo-liberal believes that gross disparities of income are inevitable. The power of transnational corporations over national governments is accepted as progress and often celebrated because it breaks down 'barriers' between peoples. The pseudo-liberal, unlike the genuine socialist (insofar as he still exists), approves of globalisation, believes that we live in a 'runaway world'. Such developments he see as positive, because they erode national consciousness, challenge traditional attitudes to family and community, and promote a purely materialistic version of politics, based on instant gratification. Pseudo-liberalism thus combines the Marxist emphasis on collective struggle with a stridently capitalist emphasis on consumer demand. Its chosen constituencies are viewed at once as classes to be emancipated, Marxist-style, and groups of consumers to be 'targeted' on quasi-commercial lines.

Marxists, and ethical socialists, have grappled with difficulty to describe what the classless society might be like and how humanity might get there. Pseudo-liberals, however, seldom attempt coherently to define 'equality', although they devote reams of copy to defining 'discrimination' and suggesting ways to ban it. The Marxist sees the classless society as the product of a scientific process, based on a rational assessment of man and history. His hesitancy about describing the ideal society is akin to the scientist's caution in talking about an experiment, even when the conclusion is virtually foregone. The Marxist's strictly scientific, in many ways over-rational, approach to politics is quite distinct from the pseudo-liberal's obeisance to unreason. Likewise, the orthodox Marxist is usually a convinced Eurocentric. He believes strongly in Western ideas of progress and rationality, rejecting pseudo-liberal assertions of Third World cultural supremacy. The Marxist analysis is rigorous and demanding. It scorns the sentimental nature worship characteristic of 'ecofeminism', along with some of the cultures associated with therapy, counselling and 'self-fulfilment', which form part of the pseudo-liberal ethos. Pseudo-liberalism appropriates elements of Marxism, in particular the idea of a society based on struggle. Yet its attack on reason and scientific method cannot be understood in Marxist terms. No genuine Marxist, for instance, would use the following arguments to attack Western science:

> Scientists must understand and struggle against the undemocratic nature of science as an institution (its hierarchy – all power to the professors. its elitism – all power to the experts. its sexism – all power to the men. and its racism – all power to the Western modes of thought).[8]

These words were penned three decades ago by Steven Rose, then Professor of Biology at the Open University and now a well-known commentator on medical ethics. At that time, pseudo-liberalism as an ideology was only beginning to take shape, emerging under the shadow of the New Left and the failure of the student revolts in 1968. From the New Left, pseudo-liberalism inherits its detestation of hierarchy, identified increasingly over the years with male authority and even with masculinity itself. It inherits an obsessive hostility to racism (but only white racism) and identification with Third World peoples in their struggle against the West. But the New Left still adhered to a Marxist analysis of society and a belief that capitalism would inevitably give way to socialism. Unlike orthodox Marxists, its campaigners perceived that the West's working class had lost a crucial element of revolutionary potential through affluence, and so the arena of struggle had shifted to Africa, Asia and Latin America. They believed that the largely peasant populations of these regions held the key to world revolution, allied to certain 'marginal' forces in the West, such as minority racial groups and students (feminists and 'gays' came later).

Pseudo-liberals retain the New Left's identification with Third World causes, although they have almost entirely jettisoned the idea of Marxist revolution, viewing globalisation and 'the market' as more efficient instruments of change. Their Third Worldism is sentimental and deceptive. At one level, it offers convenient cover for an attack on Western rationalism, promoting the idea that non-Western cultures are less rational, less patriarchal and inherently closer to nature, an idea that is itself patronising and racist. Pseudo-liberals have an emotional attachment to non-Western cultures, but only as abstractions, or rather as weapons against those elements of Western culture which stand in their way. The reality of those cultures matters less than the myths they reinforce about 'imperialism' and their propaganda value to causes like feminism or green politics. Pseudo-liberal 'anti-imperialism' is therefore more accurately described as counter-imperialism or imperialism in reverse.

The true attitude of pseudo-liberals becomes apparent when they are confronted with the politically incorrect attitudes of traditional societies outside the immediate Western orbit. Cultural relativism is swiftly cast aside in favour of a new form of moral absolutism based on 'gender equality', 'reproductive rights' and 'Equal Opportunities'. To impose this new ideology, a neo-missionary movement is created, making copious use of Western government aid and the international charity. The secular missionaries of political correctness are far more uncompromising and zealous than their religious ancestors, many of whom were restrained by the belief that they were imperfect before God. Like the missionaries of old, however, they ally themselves with modernising elites against the most conservative and religious elements within Third World societies. Their gospel of social change is closely allied to the promotion of continuous economic change. Just as the benighted natives deserve the benefits of Western feminism, so they should also receive the benefits of urbanisation, economic growth and 'market forces', the latter also acquiring semi-mystical connotations. Thus rhetorical support for non-Western cultures gives way to an evangelical desire to transform them.

Equally duplicitous is the pseudo-liberal approach to ethnic and cultural minorities within Western societies. In the strident rhetoric of 'anti-racism', there remain vestiges of the 1960s culture of protest. For the New Left, as a movement, consisted mainly of the children of the affluent society. As students and young professionals, they were beneficiaries of the Welfare State they derided and the reformist social democracy they reviled. In the United States, the anti-War protesters benefited from a selective military draft that made it easy for them to evade call-up, unlike black, Hispanic and poor white young men, with whom earlier generations of leftists would have been concerned. The iniquity and racism of the draft is rarely denounced by those who, for otherwise good reasons, campaigned against the war in Vietnam. In Britain, student activists were usually the products of selective grammar schools, which (having benefited from them) they denounced as 'elitist' and strove to destroy. In both countries, the lower-middle class nature of the New Left was reflected in its attitude towards white working people. It was an attitude of puritanical priggishness, moral disapproval, a sense of social and intellectual superiority coupled with pretensions to higher insight.

Taking their cue from Herbert Marcuse, the New Left's *eminence rouge*, the student movement rationalised anti-working class snobbery and anti-white racism. The white working-class, they claimed, had been co-opted by economic reform. It had sold out to materialism and lost its political consciousness. It was, as Marcuse argued, no longer a 'revolutionary class'. This was a useful position for New Left activists, because it enabled them to avoid the painstaking work of persuading working-class people to support them. The fact that their views were (and still are) rejected by the overwhelming majority of workers was no longer politically relevant, because those workers were suffering from 'false consciousness'. The idea that white working class people were no longer 'agents of change' also absolved middle-class leftists from residual feelings of guilt about their social snobbery. It left them free to condemn the white working-class as reactionary, backward-looking and racialist when they opposed 'liberal' ideas imposed from above and complained that they had not been consulted about the immigration policies that were transforming their neighbourhoods and threatening their economic well-being.

Thus the 'anti-racist' movement, initiated by the New Left and now one of the staples of pseudo-liberalism, is an anti-working class movement, founded on highly developed social and racial prejudices. 'Anti-racists' claim to be part of a left-wing tradition, but they are useful allies of conservative and *laissez faire* politicians who see in shifts of population useful sources of cheap labour and who are untouched personally by immigration's social costs. The 'anti-racist' movement has nothing to do with socialist politics, which have historically (and for obvious reasons) been opposed to large-scale immigration. Nor is it rooted in reason or tolerance. Instead, it is a strident, evangelical campaign, simultaneously preaching to the despised white masses (be "multicultural" or else) and using the state to impose their will. 'Anti-racism' is petty bourgeois moralism in a modern form, an excuse to treat the white working class as if they were a lower stratum of humanity or (in missionary terms) deprived natives in need of redemption. The 'anti-racist' campaigners who march self-righteously through working-class neighbourhoods, who pass 'hate crime' laws which discriminate against the white majority, who persecute opponents of multiculturalism and strive to ban from the language words they dislike belong to no credible socialist tradition. Instead, they are the true heirs of the temperance campaigners and prohibitionists who in previous generations aimed to reform the working man, first by cajoling him, then by passing oppressive laws. The dogma of multiculturalism owes nothing to the socialist analysis of society, but its censorious fervour closely resembles that of evangelical Protestantism. 'Anti-racism' is the latest manifestation of the Non-Conformist conscience. Like that brand of religiosity, it creates cowards and undermines freedom.

'Anti-racism' is the model for other pseudo-liberal campaigns, including feminism and gay rights, because of its righteous anger and its pretence of acting on behalf of the downtrodden. Like these other forms of pseudo-liberalism, it speaks with forked tongue. 'Anti-racists' claim vociferously to be on the side of black people, but their real motive is hostility towards working-class whites. To them, Ethnic Minorities are significant as an abstraction, not as real human beings. Just as Equal Opportunities are now about group entitlements rather than individual well-being, 'anti-racism' is about perpetuating racial divisions rather than transcending them. Its black opponents are denounced, with vitriol, as traitors to 'their' group. Repeatedly, pseudo-liberals voice their demands for ethnic 'diversity': in employment, political appointments, the media and the arts. Yet through this diversity, they mean to enforce conformity of thought. This is because only those who support the pseudo-liberal agenda are to be offered preferment. Only they, it is believed, represent the group, only they are true Ethnic Minorities.

Minority status, therefore, has to be earned through acceptance of political correctness and gratitude to activist groups. The movements towards group patronage (known euphemistically as 'Equal Opportunities') and group rights (through 'anti-racist' or 'anti-sexist' campaigns) mark a shift away from the traditional priorities of the left. Unlike Marxism, group rights ideology takes racial or sexual characteristics as its starting point, rather than class or economics. Unlike non-Marxist socialism, it aims to balkanise the population, rather than unite it in a common project. And unlike traditional liberalism, it is quite unconcerned with rational debate and compromise with opponents. Yet the most striking feature of pseudo-liberalism is that the move towards group rights corresponds with a move away from demands for social justice in the wider sense. In other words, addressing the grievances of groups takes precedence over a larger project, fairness to all citizens. The promotion of a group mentality, in place of shared citizenship, leads to a narrowing of political discourse and an absence of a unifying social vision. To paraphrase Margaret Thatcher, there is 'no such thing as society' under pseudo-liberalism. This does not mean that 'individuals and their families' are liberated, as she went on to suggest. Instead, there is a process of fragmentation, whereby semi-tribal group loyalty replaces civic culture whilst materialism destroys communal endeavour. This loss of respect between individuals and trust between groups serves well the agenda of market fundamentalism. Racial and sexual politics divert attention from such critical issues as insecurity at work, the distribution of wealth and the growing power of corporations. Speaking of the rise of pseudo-liberal 'identity politics' in the United States, the economist Michael J. Piore observes:

> Strong organizations and group affinities based on sex, sexual preference, racial and ethnic ties, religion, physical handicap ... have severely compromised the status of trade unions. Federal labor ... has substituted legislative remedies to the particular grievances of ... groups for collective bargaining, and in the process has encouraged people to define their grievances and to organize in that way.[9]

All these identities can be used to hide considerations of economic power or social status. Here, Priore also cites a precedent in American labour history. In the nineteenth and early twentieth centuries employers in mass production industries apportioned jobs according to the workers' ethnic origins. This was to forestall trade union organisation in a form that united the whole workforce. Loyalty to ethnic group transcended class solidarity.[10] This strategy resembles the current mania for 'diversity at work', whereby the notion of fair employment of individuals, because of their skills and dedication yields to demands for group representation ('more women 'more ethnic minorities', 'more youth' etc., instead of 'the best people for the job'). The diversity game, as it is sometimes known, reflects the pseudo-liberal view of the state as adjudicator between aggrieved groups. It is therefore embraced most fervently by government agencies where pseudo-liberal values hold sway. However it also sits well with a form of free-market dogma that is as contemptuous of tradition as the politically correct movements, regards social solidarity as outmoded and seeks to divide society into marketing niches, which largely match the pseudo-liberal groups.

Large corporations, multinationals especially, have absorbed the agendas of group rights. Their glossy propaganda brochures make a point of depicting employees of both sexes and varying racial backgrounds, smiling vapidly as they pledge loyalty to the corporate ethos, instead of to old-fashioned notions such as country or class. Such companies have Equal Opportunities policies based on group entitlement and expressed in politically correct jargon. They condone the bullying by the state of smaller businesses that cannot afford such policies or do not wish to have them. In his analysis of the decline of American left, Todd Gitlin notes the role of corporations in promoting identities politics – as a substitute for organised labour:

> No idle bystanders to social trends, many companies encourage the growth of particularist organizations in the workplace – one example is the anti-union Digital Equipment Corporation, which cultivates groups of women, blacks, and gays, to the point of buying a corporate page in the program of the Boston Gay Rights parade.[11]

Such sponsorship is commonplace in Britain, too, but not always straightforward. When United Airlines sponsored the London Gay Pride festival in 1998, they aroused the wrath of gay militants. This was because their pension scheme did not give equality to homosexual and heterosexual partnerships. In 2000, the Equal Opportunities

Commission promised to issue guidelines to employers recommending the setting up of 'lesbian and gay' groups in the workplace. What happens to those homosexuals who show no interest in such groups is not revealed. Trade unions, meanwhile, determined to banish the cloth cap image and (above all) appear less masculine, have swallowed the group rights agenda hook, line and sinker. The Association of University Teachers, for example, contains separate groups for women, 'blacks' and 'lesbians and gays'.[12] Translated, 'women' means feminists and 'black' means anyone who is not white European. The absurdity of combining male and female homosexuals has been referred to above. In any case, the doctrine of group rights separates the left from its historic commitment to a more just society for all. Although far from individualistic, it encourages petty materialism and short-term demand. Group rights destroy the possibility of a society based on trust, compassion or give-and-take. Their rise, and the decline of good manners, are part and parcel of the same process: the dismembering of our civic culture.

The premise of pseudo-liberalism, that every area of life is political, has profoundly affected relationships between people, whether in formal, social or even intimate settings. Inherited from Marxism is the idea of perpetual conflict, but the arena has shifted from economics to relations between the sexes, between parents and children or teachers and students, between ethnic groups vying for rights and between homosexuals and heterosexuals. The idea of group rights cuts across more traditional or more social forms, such as family ties, friendship, professional ethos or membership of a local community. If the purpose of life, apart from acquiring material possessions, is the assertion of rights and never-ending pursuit of equality, then there is little room for sociability, kindness or a sense of honour. Pseudo-liberals claim to be optimistic about human nature, yet theirs is ultimately a bleak vision, devoid of spiritual content, mechanical rather than rational, inflexible and ungenerous beneath a 'caring' facade. In pseudo-liberal thinking, legalistic notions take the place of moral restraints, or culturally acquired notions of good behaviour. Children, for instance, become a group with rights, rather than individuals to whom adults have obligations. The unbalanced emphasis on rights increases, and makes political, the natural conflict that arises between generations. It encourages unreasonable behaviour by children and adult irresponsibility, too. Whilst children do have rights, and must be protected by law, to view the adult-child relationship exclusively in those terms is to misunderstand human behaviour and undermine the values on which childrens' security depends. As early as 1971, the educationalist and psychotherapist Mary Miles described the inflammatory publication *Little Red Schoolbook* in these terms:

> To me, ... it seemed essentially to promote enmity between children and teachers, and my experience is that teaching and learning can only take place within a co-operative relationship.[13]

The Little Red Schoolbook was originally published in Denmark in 1969 and introduced to Britain at the beginning of the 1970s, at a time when the revolutionary New Left was already taking on the characteristics of with pseudo-liberalism.[14] It begins, in mock-Maoist style, by announcing that 'All grown-ups are paper tigers', then goes on to instruct children on how to claim their 'rights' at school by organising unions, engaging in strike action and informing against their teachers. Otherwise, the *Schoolbook* sets out a chilling summary of the pseudo-liberal agenda for education and society, which would have so much influence over the next thirty years. It opposes selective schools, exams, marks, school uniform and even sitting in rows of desks. It is critical of youth clubs, because they 'try to encourage you to have "good leisure interests"'.[15] Scout Troops are vilified for 'want[ing] to put you in uniform and control your associations with the opposite sex'.[16] Sports clubs 'teach you that what is important is to be the fastest, the strongest and always to beat other people. And to keep your mouth shut when you lose'.[17] Unsurprisingly, Army Cadet Corps are singled out for special denigration:

> Like toy guns and soldiers, war films and so many other things in our society, these organisations reinforce the idea that war is at least necessary, if not actually a good thing.[18]

The *Schoolbook* is fanatically supportive of comprehensive schools and co-education, which is considered more 'natural'. This might well be so, indeed it probably is in most circumstances and for most children. Yet as an assertion in the *Schoolbook*, it rides roughshod over individual differences of temperament, alternative educational theories and cultural differences, all of which would favour selective or single-sex schools for some children. The *Schoolbook* is therefore as doctrinaire in its prescriptions as the most narrow-minded of the 'dyed-in-the-wool' traditionalists it takes to task. Curiously for an anti-authoritarian tract, it is slavishly deferential to those in authority who impose 'change'. The feminist agenda is there, too, with the charge that schools 'discriminate against girls' and the injunction to female pupils to assert their 'rights'. Yet it is also admitted that fifty per cent more women teach in state schools than men, which suggests that there was already an anti-masculine bias in education. Private schools are condemned as elitist and 'privileged', and yet their educational methods are denigrated as backward.

All the logical inconsistencies of pseudo-liberalism are therefore present and (politically) correct. There is no notion of adult authority based on trust, of children's obedience based on respect rather than fear. Nor is it understood that competitive sports can be helpful to many pupils, including the less academic, and that military training is about service and character development, not just 'learning to kill'. As with most educational 'progressives', there is a superficial pretence of tolerance, but it is clear that children who like sport, boys who collect toy soldiers and girls or boys who take dancing classes have little right to exist, and still less right to pursue their hobbies in peace.[19] The *Schoolbook's* aversion to excellence and promotion of mediocrity, its sneering at peaceful and worthwhile activities, especially for boys, its evangelical promotion of early sex[20] have all become familiar pseudo-liberal themes, and have inflicted much misery in the process. This view of humanity and society does indeed promote enmity. It creates unhappiness, anxiety and distrust. In the same way as childhood is politicised, and so degraded, relations between the sexes become increasingly a political struggle. In the interests of 'equality', feminists promote rudeness by women to men. They condemn as patronising and 'sexist' such respectful customs as holding doors open for women, or standing when they enter a room.[21] In condemning good manners as discriminatory, and fostering bitter male-female competition, they remove the conventions which socialise young men and which make them considerate towards women. Thus they contribute to the coarsening of society, and to the cruel and violent behaviour which they vociferously condemn. Brian Mitchell, an American commentator notes, the feminist movement's double standards regarding male behaviour, and sees it as one of the corrupting effects of 'feminising' the American military:

It is a lie that the victimization of women is a product of a patriarchal culture that distinguishes male from female and orders them appropriately. The truth is that women are most victimized where they are most liberated. It is the modern world that sets the sexes at odds, that teaches boys to muscle girls on the court and on the field, that forces men to see women only as competitors and opponents. In the patriarchal world of old, the strong were obliged to serve the weak. Men and women strove to be gentlemen and ladies. Men were taught to protect women, to bear a woman's burdens, and to watch their language in her presence. Chivalry honored women with care and safety if not with freedom, at least not the freedom to be men. Today, women are free to live as coarsely and as brutally as men, while men are desensitized to the suffering of women in training. Yet, somehow, when women discern the slightest offense, the old ways are always to blame.[22]

As always, the liberation offered by pseudo-liberal values is shallow and self-defeating. Freed from the moral constraints of old-fashioned chivalry, men can be coarse, inconsiderate and irresponsible towards women. Unsocialised, they can be anti-social, deprived of male role models, they can be violent and disruptive rather than protective and loyal. Pseudo-liberalism, in short, allows men to fulfil the worst feminist prophecies, to be destructive towards themselves and others. Women, superficially liberated from men, are vulnerable to desertion and disloyalty. Pseudo-liberal cultural influence banishes the vocabulary of kindness and tact and puts in its place the language of retribution. It produces a post-modern Hobbesian savagery: a war of every woman against every man. And *vice versa*, of course. For a men's rights movement, based in London, echoes the feminist campaign against chivalry. Good manners should not be restored, because they violate egalitarian principles:

> Traditional privileges granted to women by our Society are so long-established that they are taken for granted. No-one bothers to query the right of women to take the first place in the life boat of a sinking ship, for example, or even comments on the fact that they receive their state pension at an earlier age. In theory, legislation aimed at equality would remove these privileges, in practice, they have been extended.[23]

A society of equals is, by such reasoning, a society of boors. The idea that male deference to women is good for male self-respect is alien to this new breed of activist, who owes more to feminist discourse than he cares to admit. For the struggle towards a mythical equality takes precedence over practical steps to restore balance between the sexes. Pseudo-liberalism is rarely concerned with resolving problems. Instead, it thrives on negative reactions and turns conflict into hatred. Just as feminist campaigns create enmity between the sexes, the dogmas of multiculturalism incite distrust between ethnic groups. This is because a scramble for rights and entitlements replaces ideals of generosity and open-mindedness. For homosexuals, too, the option of quiet discretion is steadily removed, berated as lack of openness or treachery to the mythic 'community'. The relentless activism of gay pressure groups makes neutrality less possible. Increasingly, judicious tolerance by heterosexuals is interpreted as a subtle form of prejudice. The liberation of homosexuals is seen as an ethical revolution, in which everyone is compelled to take sides. When homosexuals and heterosexuals are treated differently in any sense, the revolution has been betrayed. Those homosexuals who show no interest in being liberated are treated as counter-revolutionaries and collaborators.

Pseudo-liberalism takes no account of the complexities of moral debate, or the difficult choices which individuals make in their daily lives. It is oblivious to considerations of tact, or the notion that civilised relations between people often depends on what is not said. Whatever the issue, the pseudo-liberal agenda is not about co-operation, but about intensifying conflict. From unorthodox Marxism, pseudo-liberals inherit the idea of permanent revolution and implacable hatred of tradition. However, unlike adherents of Trotsky or Mao, they have little concept of what the revolution is intended to bring about. Indeed the pseudo-liberal myth of equality has much in common with the fascistic myth of racial destiny, or the anarcho-syndicalist myth of the 'General Strike'. Like these earlier forms of political correctness, pseudo-liberalism relies on unchecked emotion, sentimentality and myth. It has no concept of the individual. Like them, it places the group before the individual, supports restrictions on freedom of speech or association where these freedoms conflict with 'politically correct' goals and is prepared to use force in place of argument.

'Political correctness' has become the practical expression of pseudo-liberalism. The term reflects, in ironic manner, the obsession with 'correct' language towards or 'correct treatment' of 'oppressed groups' that characterises pseudo-liberal activities and propaganda.

This obsession makes pseudo-liberalism dangerous in three ways, which are closely connected to each other. First, its censorious, puritanical tone and tyrannical social engineering triggers intolerant backlashes against those 'groups' favoured by the politically correct. Secondly, it arouses great hostility to liberalism itself, and with it the notions of fair-mindedness and justice on which a free society is founded. Thirdly, it undermines citizenship as a common bond, uniting people of different backgrounds, interests and situations. It breaks up the population, arbitrarily, into 'groups' based on abstract characteristics, such as skin colour or sexual orientation, rather than inherited loyalties, such as to family or region, or to chosen loyalties, such as to profession or hobby. The process of classifying individuals is central to pseudo-liberalism. It perpetuates, often wilfully, the very divisions it is claiming to heal.

Like other totalitarian movements, pseudo-liberalism has depended for its success on its opponents' failure of nerve. The pseudo-conservatism diagnosed by Adorno and colleagues became a mass movement in 1930s Germany in part because of the absence of a systematic conservative critique. Confused by the destruction of familiar symbols of authority, disbelieving in the legitimacy of the Weimar Republic, and frightened by Communism's appeal, some German conservatives hoped that they could use the Nazi movement to restore their values. Its vulgarity eventually appalled them, and its contempt for human life surpassed their most dire expectations. Liberal surrender to pseudo-liberal campaigns often resembles conservative surrender to the extreme right. Pseudo-liberal campaigners appeal to liberals' belief in human progress and concern for justice. When they are weak, they emphasise 'tolerance', one of the founding principles of liberal thought. When they are more confident, they call for 'action' and label those who dissent as reactionaries. When they are strong, they use the state to restrict the freedoms of others and the education system to indoctrinate the young. It is then that the authoritarian nature of political correctness becomes apparent, even to many of its erstwhile champions.

Liberal values of freedom and tolerance have strong roots in Britain and the United States. They are adhered to there, and in much of Europe, by the majority of the population, who would not necessarily describe themselves as 'liberals'. Yet true liberalism has come increasingly to be the creed of the apolitical. It is reflected in conversations between friends and neighbours, in talks between strangers in pubs and cafes, in jokes told in coffee breaks at work, in all voluntary activities that bring people together. It is reflected in the persistence of all-male groups, as natural formations, despite propaganda and coercive attempts at 'gender integration'. Some of these groups are peaceful and productive, such as clubs for working or professional men. Others, like criminal gangs or football thugs, display a darker side, not of masculinity itself, but of a society that fails to recognise male energy or properly socialise its young men. In short, they are uninitiated warriors, deprived of a chivalrous ethic, bereft of a community to serve.

Contempt – often vehement – for political correctness is one of the few potential sources of political unity. It cuts across traditional barriers of region, class and race, the barriers which pseudo-liberals rage against but in practice reinforce. Pseudo-liberalism expresses itself through movements so alien to the wishes of the majority that a reaction against it is already beginning. To ensure that this reaction is a tolerant one, instead of simply reactionary', politicians of courage and dignity are needed. They should remind us that we are robust individuals still able to think for ourselves, who can and must restore tolerance and fair play.

6. Unisexism: The Politics of Emasculation

The unquestioned acceptance of feminist goals has become almost universal in Western political and intellectual life, at least in the politics and ideas that dare speak their name.[1] That is not to say that the populations of Western nations have been converted to feminism *en masse*. On the contrary, radical feminism and, all too often, radical feminists themselves are probably more objects of ridicule than ever before, by women at least as much as by men. That ridicule is now accentuated by fear. Fear stems from an awareness of the power that feminist ideology exerts over academics, educators, policy-makers and the media, over those who make intimate decisions about other people's lives, such as doctors and social workers, or those who interpret and enforce the law. It explains the tendency of institutions, including highly traditional institutions, to give in to feminism and become vehicles for dogmatic social engineering. 'I am a feminist,' protests the conservative commentator.

'I am not a sexist,' the Anglican traditionalist assures his critics. 'Of course "equal opportunity" is a good thing,' declares the Infantry officer, defensively. Such protestations effectively neutralise moral arguments for the traditional family, theological arguments against the ordination of women, or the case for the all-male regiment, with the pride, stability and *esprit de corps* that it engenders. Thus important and valuable arguments are being lost before they even begin. This has nothing to do with whether they are right or wrong. For each of the arguments I have listed raises distinctive questions, moral, social and in one case theological. They can be resolved, therefore, only as individual problems on a case-by-case basis, not in the context of an abstract, all-embracing doctrine of equality. But as soon as the word equality is mentioned, feminism's opponents suffer a failure of nerve.

That failure of nerve has several powerful cultural and political causes. One of these is the feminists' manipulation of the ideal of male chivalry, although they decry it as chauvinistic and outdated. At a personal level, feminists play shamelessly upon a man's wish, both natural and nurtured, to treat women with politeness and respect, and to concede graciously to their interests or requirements. The impotence of many men in authority when confronted with feminist demands for change stems from those very traditions of male courtesy which feminists disparage. When a man of tolerant disposition is browbeaten into believing that feminists 'represent' *all* women, and that failure to 'include' women or give them preferment over other men is hurtful or downright cruel, then he is more or less destined to surrender. This is why many of feminism's most effective opponents have been women rather than men. They know from their experiences and observations that feminist ideology is laughably out of tune with most women's priorities and needs. Unfettered by male chivalry, they can voice their opposition clearly and logically, or give vent to their anger without constraint.[2]

The significance of the abuse of chivalry should not be underestimated. It informs decisions made every day in business, politics, the media and institutions of learning at all levels. In personal terms, therefore, feminists profit from the survival of traditional patterns of behaviour and thought. They benefit, too, from having a 'total' view of the world, which their opponents generally lack. That is to say, they believe that all aspects of life are intimately connected and that these connections are all entirely political. The opponent of feminism, by contrast, is likely to draw distinctions between his working life, his family life and his private hobbies. There might be overlaps, but they are nonetheless distinctive parts of his life and are judged by different criteria. The feminist draws no such distinctions, her (or his) world view pithily encapsulated in the assertion that 'the personal is political'.

The fear of being different is another powerful deterrent to opposition, and is perhaps especially marked amongst intellectuals. Part of this is cowardice. When George Orwell described his contemporaries as 'the pansy left', he was not referring to the sexual orientations of his literary colleagues, as much as their lack of intellectual virility. They had refused to open their eyes to the totalitarian nightmare that was Soviet Communism because it was easier and more convenient to 'fellow travel'. Yet there is more to it than that.

One aspect of the Western intellectual tradition has always been reductionism, the desire to level humanity, society and nature to a series of simple formulae and so 'resolve' the human predicament. This explains the recent popularity, amongst modern intellectuals, of totalitarian movements, be they left or right, just as inflexible religious dogmas prevailed amongst their scholarly forebears and Idealist schools inspired the learned men of antiquity.

Opposed to this is a rival, parallel tradition of critical thought, questioning and fearless, unfettered discussion. Although never wholly secure, this tradition of freedom has given Western culture its dynamism. It has been the source of our great literature and art, of our exploratory instincts, scientific inquiry and capacity for reasoning, achievements now denigrated by feminist ideology as 'patriarchal' and 'male-dominated'. The Western sense of freedom is rooted in respect for the individual. As such, it acknowledges the complexities of the human experience and opposes all forms of fanaticism. It has stood, with varying degrees of success, between Western man and those grand designs that threaten the balance between the individual and society, tradition and change, reform and continuity.

That sense of freedom Tocqueville rightly described as 'the sacred flame of liberty'. In the West today, it is more 'scared' than 'sacred' and it is remarkable that it continues to burn even faintly. Free thinking can take place only in an atmosphere of confidence. That means confidence in the *underlying* values of a society and the confidence which the individual has in himself. The former is under attack from the ideology of 'multiculturalism' which, turning old-fashioned prejudice on its head equates the pursuit of truth, individual freedom and rational thought with white supremacy. In the political sphere, multiculturalists abolish the idea of equality for all individuals under the rule of law and replace it with special privileges for groups: reverse racism, known as 'affirmative action' and 'hate crime' legislation, which amounts to a form of 'affirmative lynch law'. Academic multiculturalists, where possible, impose curricula based on a know-nothing, think-nothing cultural relativism that regards the slogans of Algerian terrorists and the thoughts of Greek philosophers as equally 'valid', but brooks no opposition to egalitarian doctrines. This mentality is typified by Reverend Jesse Jackson leading a band of student activists around Stanford University in the early 1990s chanting 'Hey, hey, ho, ho, Western Civilisation's got to go!'[3]

Jackson's own career has been built on the continued existence of racism and black poverty.

Feminists ally themselves with multiculturalists in their generalised attack on freedom of thought, freedom of speech and freedom of association. Like multiculturalists, they attack 'Western culture'[4] for valuing reason over intuition and for pursuing objectivity rather than merely accepting subjectivity. Where multiculturalists interpret these qualities as 'white' and inferior, feminists interpret them as 'male' and unconscionable. However, feminism itself quickly assumes racialist, indeed imperialist, overtones in its overt contempt for non-Western societies and the role of women within them, in its insistence that there is only one path to 'equality' and that it is secular, materialistic and careerist. Feminism soon sheds its 'multicultural' rhetoric when it confronts traditional structures such as arranged marriages and the extended family, or cultures which revere motherhood over work outside the home. Women from traditional societies are not asked whether or not they wish to be 'liberated' by feminist social policy. It is believed, by the new missionaries of 'reproductive rights' and paid employment that they must change, whether they want to or not. Feminist values, therefore, play a pivotal role in the process of 'globalisation', economic and cultural. They seek to abolish traditional attitudes towards the family and work, and with them patterns of behaviour that challenge corporate dominance and uncritical consumerism.

Allied to the multiculturalist attack on individual freedom and cultural confidence is a system of education which increasingly favours conformity over individuality, sociability over idiosyncrasy and passive 'socialisation' over original thought. Although allegedly 'progressive' and centred upon the individual, the overwhelming thrust of modern mass education is towards persuading the individual to conform. Unlike more traditional educational methods that are defamed as oppressive, it favours levelled-down consensus over individualistic argument and replaces discipline and moral guidance with forms of therapy and counselling that foster conformist attitudes. The superficial freedom afforded by the modern school or college – absence of uniform, dress code or rigid rules; stress on sexual egalitarianism – conceals a more 'censored' environment than that of a traditional boys' boarding school. There is little institutional ethos, but there is peer pressure supported by a perpetually benign yet stifling authority structure. There is little organised religious observance – at least nothing with any dangerous spiritual content – but the gospel of equality is preached assiduously at all levels. Eccentricity, that great humanising force, is discouraged, amongst educators and educated alike, for 'tolerance' is a virtue only when extended to groups, not to individuals who think differently. There are few formal rules, but a system of values that encourages quiet obedience (educational and behavioural), memorising rather than thinking for oneself, co-operation rather than individual discovery.

Modern education, in short, provides a system that seems to favour traditionally female values of restraint over traditionally masculine values of exploration, independence and physical energy. This is indeed ironic, given that one of the purposes of 'progressive' education was to break down differences between the sexes, which were thought to be culturally conditioned rather than influenced by biology. Feminists tend strongly to support this education in sentimentality, largely because they believe that it will have an emasculating effect on men. Rewarding passive conformity and imposing pacific values certainly has the effect of alienating large numbers of physically and mentally healthy young men, along with a good number of spirited young women, too. The energies of these young people are, from an early stage, diverted from the pursuit of knowledge and towards less fruitful ways of questioning authority. Young men who lack male mentors and are offered 'counselling' in place of more traditional forms of character training will tend to rebel against this tyranny of Compulsory Niceness. With the decline of manufacturing industry and the growing 'political correctness' and loss of status of the Armed Forces, they have fewer constructive outlets for their naturally rebellious energy. This vacuum is filled increasingly by bullying, crime, alcoholism and drug abuse. Further education – and academic life in general – becomes attractive to young people whose instinct is to absorb and accept, rather than argue and think.

In *The Lonely Crowd*, David Riesman and his colleagues describe the educational impact of the social transition they identify in midtwentieth century American society: from 'inner-direction', where the individual draws upon his inner resources, and 'other-direction', by which individuals derive their values from their peers. They show that 'progressive' schooling in American cities has proved instrumental in that transition. As the emphasis shifted from formality to informality, single sex to co-ed classes, pure academic education to 'nurturing', a new pattern of conformity was imposed, one more extreme than the old because rebellion against it was well-nigh impossible[5]:

> The effort is to cut everyone down to size who stands up or stands out in any direction. Beginning with the very young and going on from there, overt vanity is treated as one of the worst offenses, as perhaps dishonesty would have been in an earlier day. Being high-hat is forbidden.
>
> Temper, manifest jealousy, moodiness – these, too, are offenses in the code of the peer-group. All 'knobbly' or idiosyncratic qualities are more or less systematically repressed. And judgment of others by peer-group members are so clearly matters of taste that their expression has to resort to the vaguest phrases, constantly changed: cute, lousy, square, etc. ...
>
> But to say that judgments of peer-groupers are matters of taste, not of morality or even opportunism, is not to say that any particular child can afford to ignore these judgements. One the contrary, he is, as never before, at their mercy. If the peer-group were – and we continue to deal here with the urban middle classes only – a wild, torturing, obviously vicious group, the individual child might still feel moral indignation as a defense against its commands. But like adult authorities in the other-directed socialization process, the peer-group is friendly and tolerant. It stresses fair play, Its conditions for entry seem reasonable and well meaning. But even where this is not so, moral indignation is out of fashion. The child is therefore exposed to trial by jury without any defenses either from the side of its own morality or from the adults. All the morality is the group's.[6]

The Lonely Crowd was first published half a century ago. Since then, the 'progressive' ethos of Compulsory Niceness has pervaded higher, as well as primary and secondary, education. It is the system of values against which most public policies are measured. Compulsory Niceness is an institutionalised failure of nerve. Its quest for bland consensus does not favour genuine moderation, which is intellectually rigorous and uncompromising. Instead, it provides a backdrop of messy compromise, against which fanatics of various kinds can play out their ideological dramas. It is marked, too, by a diminution in the importance of the autonomous individual. Government is seen, increasingly, as a mediator between groups claiming rights at the expense of other groups, or the rest of society. Where these groups are presented as 'disadvantaged', or having suffered in the past, opposition to their demands is seen as a form of bad manners, or as an implicit act of cruelty. It is, quite literally, 'not nice' to be against feminism, when it is assumed that feminists speak for all 'women'. It is not nice to be against 'gay rights', if gay activists speak for all homosexuals, or against 'multiculturalism', if we accept that multiculturalists speak for all black people, or indeed all ethnic minorities. That all these propositions are manifestly untrue is a matter of inconvenience and irritation, which 'nice' people don't mention. They assume that individuals fit neatly into groups which act *en bloc*, and if for some reason they fail to do so, they must be persuaded, then coerced.[7]

There is a striking similarity between the meaningless phrases uttered by the children in Riesman's survey and the slogans of politicians and activists fifty years later. Peer group pressure defines what is 'cool' or 'neat' amongst adolescents. Amongst intellectuals, it defines the meaning of 'diversity' and 'inclusion', two of the buzzwords of Compulsory Niceness. Diversity becomes a euphemism for conformist acceptance of group rights, and hostility to those who emphasise individualism or tradition instead. Inclusion is taken to mean favouring members of acceptable groups (women, ethnic minorities, homosexuals) at the expense of unacceptable groups (men, 'white Europeans', heterosexuals) and ritually denouncing anyone who questions this process.[8] In the name of diversity and inclusion, some ideas are placed off-limits, others accorded a superstitious reverence. Two of the latter are 'progress' and 'equality'. As ideas, they are intimately connected, for one is deemed to lead logically to the other. They are both defined, in Looking-Glass terms, as whatever their supporters choose them to mean. Progress can mean curtailing freedom of speech, if that speech is deemed 'racist' or 'sexist'. Equality can mean its opposite, inequality, provided that it is inequality for groups disliked by egalitarians. To oppose progress is to be a 'reactionary', which the modern intellectual fears more than almost anything else, except being a 'bigot', which is his fate if he opposes socially engineered equality.

Feminism is the ultimate group rights ideology. Feminists present 'women' as an oppressed minority, when claiming special rights. When asserting themselves politically, they stress the numerical majority that 'women' actually make up. On behalf of 'women', they seek legal reparations against the collective 'enemy' (men) through skewed divorce laws, reverse discrimination in employment and special privileges in political representation.[9] At one level, they demand the right for women to do exactly the same things as men, in every sphere of life. At another, they claim for 'women' special insights of a spiritual or ecological nature. A movement founded on double-think, feminism thrives in a political climate where its is considered ill-mannered (or, in old-fashioned terms, ungentlemanly) to question the demands of single-issue movements. It is sustained by a culture in which equality has acquired totemic status and support for equality is a condition of entry to the intellectual peer group. Compulsory Niceness deters consideration of what kind of ideology feminism really is.

It is tempting, indeed almost compelling, to view feminism as a left-wing ideology, or as a movement that has evolved from socialism. Many on the left believe this, which is why they capitulate so easily to feminist demands even when their instincts cry out against them. It explains, too, why it is difficult to elicit opposition, or even mild criticism of feminist ideology from the political left. For surely, the principled leftist will argue, the aims of feminism are good ones, although its methods are sometimes wrong. Surely the intention of feminists is to uplift the status of women, and so we must support them, even when we disagree with their methods. To such left-wingers, accession to feminist demands is akin to support for 'progressive' dictatorships, because their authoritarian methods are merely 'instruments of transition', or because imperialist aggression makes them necessary.

For socialists of the Marxist or Fabian schools, which have more in common than is widely realised, feminism offers rich opportunities for collectivist solutions, for 'bringing the state back in' to the individual's life. For ageing New Left radicals, the 'gender' feminist programme is the latest stage in the sexual revolution. Along with its illegitimate offspring, 'gay liberation', feminism provides a virulent critique of family life which rationalises past selfishness and present disappointment. Association with its triumphs conveniently compensates for political failure. Socialists of a green, decentralist or more liberal bent see in feminism, and single-issue campaigns more generally, a humanitarian alternative to the centralised, class-based politics of the orthodox left. They believe the rhetoric of 'non-hierarchical structures' and 'leaderless coalitions' and willingly mouth sentimental slogans about 'reclaiming herstory' (as opposed to male-imposed *his*tory), 'celebrating queer culture' (homosexuals as an ersatz ethnic group) and 'embracing diversity' (patronising tokenism). To such jaded idealists, the tawdry reality of these movements is of little consequence. They fulfil a wish, perhaps a need, for continuous agitation, and they hold out faint hopes for the transformation of mankind. Critics of feminism accept its quasi-socialist credentials. The American 'neoconservative' Michael Levin, for instance, described campaigns for 'equal pay for equal work' as 'the feminist road to socialism'.[10] Erin Pizzey, who was censured and even threatened by feminists when she pointed out that women as well as men commit domestic violence, has spoken of 'radical feminists' as Marxists who have 'jumped ship'.[11]

This interpretation of feminism is understandable, given its promise of an egalitarian Utopia and its successful mimicking of socialist rhetoric. In practice, too, feminist agendas require a vast amount of state intervention in the economy and society, with the enforcement of 'Equal Opportunity' laws becoming a vast, unproductive nationalised industry. Feminist assumptions have certainly been built into Marxist political thought from the beginning, despite Marx's own apparent conservatism on such matters.[12] As early as 1854, Marx's collaborator Friedrich Engels wrote *The Origin of the Family, Private Property and the State*, in which he identified relations between the sexes with the 'antagonism' of class struggle, rather than with the human qualities of affection, loyalty or passion:

> the first class oppression that occurs in history coincides with the development of antagonism between man and woman in monogamous marriage. and the first class oppression coincides with that of the female sex by the male.[13]

Modern feminists and their male fellow travellers aim to impose their vision of equality on women who reject it as much as on men who resist it, through methods which include state coercion, vilification of critics and efforts to indoctrinate children and students. The hostility of feminists towards traditionalist women is, if anything, more virulent and ideologically charged than their hostility to men. Betty Friedan, supposedly American feminism's moderate or liberal face, described mothers who stay at home with their children as 'obsolete'. More extreme still, but with refreshing Gallic honesty, the childless Simone de Beauvoir proclaimed as early as 1975 that:

No woman should be authorised to stay at home and raise her children. Society should be totally different. Women should not have that choice, precisely because if there is such a choice, too many women will make that one.[14]

In the same dialogue with Friedan, Jean-Paul Sartre's consort defines feminism's central goal as freedom of choice. To view this position as inconsistent is to misunderstand feminist ideology. For the choice of a woman to stay at home with her young children, or to put her family life before her career, is not an authentic choice. It is based on traditionalist prejudices about the role of women, which she has 'internalised' and from which it is the duty of feminists to 'free' her. For feminists, by definition, represent 'women' and interpret their interests for them, just as an earlier Marxist generation interpreted the will of the working-class. Feminism is quietly rejected by many women and so depends on male support, much of which is achieved through emotional blackmail, such as the threat of being called 'sexist', which few 'sensitive' male liberals appreciate. In the much the same way, Marxist socialism depended on middle-class support, because it was often deeply unpopular amongst working class communities.

Male supporters of feminism are, but for a few extremists, self-conscious and uncertain. To follow feminism's correct line, they tie themselves in complicated ideological knots. When this author observed, in correspondence with a socialist, pro-feminist man, that poverty amongst women had increased dramatically after two decades of feminist social policy and the resulting family breakdown, his reply was as crisp as it was honest. 'They may be poorer,' he told me, but at least they are free from chauvinist men'. Such a romantic association of poverty and freedom seems odd for a socialist 'moderniser', resembling a certain strain of conservative thought, or a rustic anarchism long scorned by the 'progressive' left. And it fails to explain how a new morality that accepts the desertion of women by men, leaving them to bring up their children alone and in poverty, can be anything other than 'chauvinistic'. Pro-feminist men denounce traditional masculine attributes with the same zeal that some white liberals denounce 'Western civilisation' and all that flows from it, including democracy. They apologise, as if on behalf of all men, for oppressions past, present and yet to come. They pay ritual tribute to 'the women's struggle for rights, which has a long and valorous history'[15]. They make a point of saying 'his or her', or 'her or his', refusing to use the word 'man' (although 'woman' is still accept-able, for some reason) and drooling like Pavlov dogs whenever 'women's issues' are mentioned. Most do this for purely self-serving reasons, or through the failure of nerve discussed above. A few, however, display a virulent hatred of their own masculinity. Were they homosexuals, they would be denounced for 'self-hatred' by shrilly intolerant gay activists. As Robert Bly explains:

> [*Male feminists*] put forward the view that traditional masculinity authenticates itself through oppressing women. Masculinity to them is essentially toxic, like a poison.

> Traits traditionally imagined as masculine, such as competitiveness, wildness, and aggression, spring, they believe, from culture, not genetic inheritance. Since masculinity is made, it can be remade. They want a new man, and they want him now.

> Most feminist men hate the concept of "deep masculinity". The feminist writer Tim Beneke says: "There is no such thing as deep masculinity because there is no such thing as masculinity." Whatever comes out of the masculine soul is, in their view, wrong by essence.[16]

Such 'feminist men' have much in common with middle-class radicals who ostentatiously renounce the bourgeois culture that sustains them and adopt fake working class accents. Indeed, like 'female' feminists, they believe that they know 'what women want' better than most women know it themselves. Feminist ideology inherits from Marxism the theory of 'false consciousness' to which we referred in earlier chapters. Put simply, this is the notion that the worker is oppressed, even if he does not know it, or even if he is actively hostile to the idea. Those loyalties that give his life meaning, such as to a church, a regiment or a football team, are false loyalties, as is his sense of patriotism or pride in his local community. Part of the revolutionary process is to 'demystify' him, so that he becomes conscious of his oppression. For in Marxist terms, he is defined by his relationship to the means of production, not to his fellow men. For feminists, the means of production are replaced by the means of reproduction. A woman's loyalty to her sex comes before her personal tastes and preferences, her religious or moral beliefs and the relationships that give her life meaning. Feminist ideology assumes, for example, that a mother in the North of England will be more interested in 'opportunities for women' than the fate of her unemployed husband (displaced by the decline of manufacturing) or the fate of her sons in an education system that is frequently anti-male. Her love for her husband and sons is a form of 'false consciousness', which prevents her from 'asserting her rights'.

Also inherited from Marxism is the idea of an underlying struggle. For Marxists, that is the economic struggle between worker and capitalist, the class struggle, for feminists, it is a sex struggle, or 'gender war', in which the individual is required to take sides. And just as the class struggle culminates in the classless socialist society, so the sex struggle must culminate in the unisex society. Unisexism takes as its starting point two ideas. First, it insists that differences between the sexes are culturally conditioned and owe nothing to human nature, which is also seen as an artificial 'construct'. Secondly, those differences are always wrong and must always be 'challenged' and broken down. It would be mistaken to conclude from this that unisexism was about giving men and women the freedom to 'be themselves' and express their true natures as individuals. On the contrary, it seeks to impose on both sexes a revolutionary imperative of change. Males are expected to apologise, concede and repress their 'aggression', females to overthrow 'gender stereotypes'. As in socialist programmes of the old-fashioned kind, the state is looked to as the agent of change and education is seen as a means to indoctrinate the young. Thus the state has a duty to enforce unisexist precepts, to ensure that women are encouraged, or compelled, to perform the same social functions as men. Where this does not happen, 'positive action' must be taken, because the revolution has been betrayed. The married woman who stays at home is a counter-revolutionary. She and her husband should be penalised financially by the state until she makes the politically correct choice. This is why institutionalised discrimination against the stay-at-home mother has been built into government policy in Britain, the logical conclusion of years of state-directed change. In taxation, the married couple's allowance has been abolished. Low income single mothers, meanwhile, are compelled to seek work outside the home. This means that a mother who leaves her own children and is paid to look after someone else's, is considered a better citizen than one who stays with her offspring.

Feminist social policy does not discourage single motherhood, because of the relative poverty – and lack of opportunity – that it tends to produce. On the contrary, it is presented as one amongst many 'lifestyle options', along with cohabitation, 'serial monogamy' and lesbian motherhood. All these options are morally equivalent, but some are more equivalent than others. The most equivalent of all are those which demonstrate that women can live independently of men, even where that independence is artificial and leads to a form of forced marriage to the state, or dependence upon a sweatshop employer. Thus, it is politically correct to dismiss traditional marriages as reactionary, but incorrect in the extreme to criticise artificial insemination for single women.

In the interests of socially engineered equality, feminists and their supporters are obsessed with eliminating male bastions. These range from professions and professional organisations, such as Working Men's Clubs, gentlemen's clubs, sports clubs and even clubs or societies for male homosexuals. Methods vary from emotional blackmail to recourse to the courts, from invocation of 'anti-discrimination' laws to the refusal of public funds. The destruction of male bastions is considered an ethical goal in its own right, more important than the true aspirations of women.[17] In England and Wales, for example, the Fire Service has been set a 'recruitment target' of fifteen per cent more women, purely for ideological reasons. The same government report grudgingly admitted that the Service was efficient, well-liked and trusted more than any other public agency, but then attacked it for its 'male' ethos and 'militaristic culture'. Similarly, the Armed Forces are increasingly forced to take account of feminist preoccupations in their recruitment policy, their training and their disciplinary structure. The Ministry of Defence has a 'Gender Unit', the very title of which implies profound ideological bias. Its brief includes expanding areas of 'gender integration' and pressing for women to be sent to the front line. Operational efficiency has nothing to do with any of these considerations. On the contrary, it is subordinate to the dogma of 'equality', so that the very structures and traditions which have made for cohesion are wilfully undermined. The following recommendations, issued by the anti-discrimination industry to a compliant government, express well growing demands for 'feminisation':

> The Equal Opportunities Commission urges that it should be made easier for women to join the Services. The Army should recruit more of them to a wider range of posts, said Julie Mellor, the commission chairman.

"We believe that the Armed Forces are missing out on many good quality potential recruits.

"Training initiatives to equip women to work in jobs traditionally done by men would help to boost the number of women applying."

The commission says that the culture within the Services must change, so that attitudes towards women, especially those with children, do not stop them applying for jobs.[18]

The United States provides much evidence that 'gender integration' is unpopular in the Forces, and becomes a source of indiscipline and litigation. There, the process of feminisation has advanced much further than in Britain, to the extent that group rights are routinely placed above the needs of a fighting force. This makes it the model for British feminists, who loathe successful masculine cultures more than they dislike 'male violence'. The politically correct administration of the US Armed Forces is personified by Lieutenant General Claudia Kennedy, the highest ranking woman officer dubbed 'Hillary Clinton's favourite General' and centre of a high-profile 'sexual harassment case'. Criticised for her alleged closeness to the Democratic Party, General Kennedy is remembered for proclaiming to West Point cadets: 'This is not the Army your fathers joined'.[19]

On both sides of the Atlantic, the Armed Forces are used increasingly as a social laboratory. The aim of the experiment is to prove to the wider society that the traditional roles of the sexes can be transformed or reversed. Unlike a genuine scientific experiment, there is little attempt at objectivity. The response to failure is not to abandon the project, but to return to it with renewed zeal, to conclude that more 'equal opportunities training', or more 'anti-discrimination' edicts are required. In civilian life, as well as the Forces, unisex feminism sees education as the key to 'progress'. Education, in this context, does not mean the quest for knowledge, but propaganda techniques that call to mind the Communist regimes of Eastern Europe and China under the 'Gang of Four'. Amongst these are the censorship of traditional and much-loved children's books for alleged 'sexism', alongside other bugbears such as 'racism', 'imperialism' and 'militarism'. More proactive – a word beloved of social engineers – are 'social education' classes. These propagate 'anti-sexist' doctrines, and other 'politically correct' shibboleths, as if they were truths, and as if no other views of the world could ever exist. Sex education, also, is presented increasingly in terms of crude bodily functions rather than complex moral choice, with children of both sexes taught to 'role play' and some cases to experiment. They are encouraged to question the values of their parents, if they are conservative, but the permissive, hedonistic approach is held to be beyond criticism.

Such methods are justified in terms of promoting 'safer sex' or preventing teenage pregnancies. These claims are belied by statistics, which show continually rising pregnancies in girls under sixteen, along with an epidemic of sexually transmitted disease amongst young people in general. It might seem that the real objective of 'sex education' is less to inform and promote free discussion, more to break down the barriers of discretion and reserve between males and females, along with the civilisation, courtesy and mutual trust that they engender. There is also the intention that the 'patriarchal' family should disappear, because it is the originator of 'inequality'. British parents cannot withdraw their children from 'personal and social' education, even where it is a vehicle for propaganda, but they can withdraw them from religious instruction. Those teachers who oppose religion in schools, and wish to banish prayer from morning assemblies, tend also to be the strongest advocates of 'anti-sexist' or 'anti-racist' education, or instruction in 'value-free' sex – not value-free at all, but far more 'judgmental' than traditional censure. The classroom is not the place to consider anything transcendent, but it can and should be used for 'tackling gender issues' or 'eliminating sexism'.

In the United States, where state schooling is rigidly secular, feminist intervention in the curriculum is commonplace and has aroused deep antipathy. Reassuringly, perhaps, American feminists seem to possess a special talent for revealing their totalitarian instincts and exposing themselves to ridicule. Alice Rossi, for example, recommended that school outings or field trips be curtailed, for fear that 'going out into the community in this way, youngsters would observe men and women in their present occupational roles'. In the late 1970s, the [former] Department of Health, Education and Welfare reviewed children's books for indications of 'sexism'. The intention was that books aimed at children should reflect reality 'not as it was, but as it will be'. Demands persist for 'unisex' schoolbooks, pointedly showing men and women in identical roles, or better still in roles that have been reversed. Meanwhile, the feminist commentator Judith Bardwick describes the hostility of children to such attempts at brainwashing as an 'anti-feminist backlash':

> Another source of resistance to feminist goals is the conservatism of children. They seem very resistant to changing ideas about what the sexes are supposed to do and be like.[20]

The 'conservatism of children', which Bardwick condemns, arises from an instinctive, and culturally inherited sense of freedom, and a contempt for those who use positions of trust to impose alien ideologies. To feminists, it is further evidence of false consciousness, requiring more, rather than less unisexism to counter undesirable 'influences' from home, society or students thinking for themselves. Unisexism's revolutionary imperative to destroy traditional stereotypes means that, for both young women and young men, a preference for those stereotypes is not an option. If we assume that boys play with soldiers and girls with dolls simply out of 'conditioning', and that such 'conditioning' is always a bad thing, then it follows that girls should be forced to play with soldiers and boys with dolls. If we assume that there is a sex struggle, in which 'male' values are inherently oppressive, it follows that young males should be forced to conform to values identified as 'feminine'. A good example of this approach is found in a report on the future of outdoor pursuits published in Britain in the early 1980s, which despite (or perhaps because of) an all-male panel is blatantly contemptuous of the 'traditionally masculine' associations of outdoor activities. These activities are no longer seen as hobbies to be enjoyed, but as a means to fit children into unisex moulds:

> This may entail a departure from the prevalent male-oriented models of outdoor programmes. However, there may be substantial gains, not only in enabling and encouraging young women to participate more readily, but also for the young men to experience a different way of living and behaving. Both boys and girls may become more aware of each other's capabilities.

> Even this level of care in designing outdoor experiences may not be sufficient to encourage some young women to participate. The appropriate answer may be to provide all-female outdoor experience.[21]

As always with unisexist programmes, some are more equal than others. There is no mention of single-sex provision for those young men who benefit more from that approach or find it preferable to 'mixed' activities. Furthermore, it is the 'young men' who are required to 'experience a different way of living', as private pursuits are turned into vehicles for social change. One result of such attempts to politicise outdoor pursuits has been to create a nation of youthful couch potatoes. The alienation of young men from activities allowing them positively to express their masculinity, and learn from older men, has made anti-social behaviour seem more attractive. The attempt to tame young men has failed abysmally, like earlier progressive attempts to banish competitive instinct altogether. Meanwhile, single-sex outdoor pursuits become increasingly a luxury, for those who can pay for them, or those who have fathers, male relatives or inspiring older male friends.

Feminism, especially when expressed through unisexist programmes, has much in common with dogmatic socialism. It is based on an abstract vision of women, and of men, which denies both individual choice and individuality itself. It attempts, with disastrous results, to transform human nature through the force of the state. Just as state socialism repudiates 'bourgeois' class distinctions, feminism denies the value of differences between the sexes, except where those differences can be used to feminist advantage. Feminists and doctrinaire socialists alike repudiate distinctions between public and private life, and establish no limits to the state's power to intervene. Both are offended by, and seek to destroy, those institutions that operate successfully on principles opposed to theirs: hierarchy, deference, all-male membership or, occasionally, all-female membership of a non-feminist nature.[22] Yet the totalitarian implications of feminist ideology need not be associated exclusively with the left. It might be more instructive to see in feminism a mutation from the socialist tradition, rather than a logical development thereof. In this sense, it bears a striking resemblance to the ideology we have come to know as fascism.

7. The Feminist Road to Fascism?

The popularity of 'anti-fascist' slogans in left-wing circles obscures the connection between fascist world-view and that of a certain form of 'unscientific' socialism. For the inspiration behind fascist movements did not come from the conservative wing of politics. Fascism instead emerged as a revolutionary movement for change, a technocratic movement favoured by Italian Futurist painters who celebrated the machine[1] and at the same time a mystical ideology, invoking race rather than citizenship or class as the source of personal and political identity. More than that, race is presented as a cosmic abstraction, in which the will of the individual is submerged and directed towards collectivist ends. In this way, the individual at once 'discovers' his true identity and loses his consciousness of himself. For the theorists of National Socialism, loyalty to the *Volk* overrode lesser loyalties, such as to family or friends. Fascist ideology in that respect resembles Marxism, which elevates 'class' above everything else in the individual's life. It also resembles feminism, which elevates 'gender' over all things.

Fascism, like modern 'political correctness', is based on group rights. These rights are exercised through the exclusion or conquest of other groups. The individual acquires rights (or loses them) through his membership of a group based on ties of blood or ethnic origin. The parallels between fascist group rights and the claims of multiculturalist ideologues are quite uncanny. For one of the ironies of multiculturalism is that it has meant that racial classifications are discussed as assiduously on the left as on the extreme right. More significantly for this discussion, fascist group rights resemble those of Marxism and feminism. They place innate loyalty to group over other, freely chosen loyalties or interests. They posit a theory of rights based on claims against other groups, and acquired through struggle. Whether it is a struggle by woman against man, worker against capitalist, or 'race and nation' against 'inferior' races, the underlying principle is antipathy to the liberal state, based on the balance between tradition and individual choice.

However unlike Marxism, but like feminism, fascist ideology exalts unreason, seeing in primitive superstition a higher truth.

Fascism's left-wing antecedents can be found largely in anarcho-syndicalism, a radical movement fashionable in Western Europe and the United States before World War I, which persisted in Spain and South America until the 1930s. Anarcho-syndicalism was a variant of revolutionary anarchism which favoured the class struggle and viewed industrial workers as agents of change. Where syndicalists and other socialists differed was in their rejection of parliamentary procedures, even as a tactical ploy. They opposed party structures as authoritarian and lacking in revolutionary purity. But crucially, anarcho-syndicalists also abhorred the 'scientific' approach of Marxist ideologues. They saw in the group dynamic of working-class organisation something beyond mere politics and economics: a form of spiritual energy. Georges Sorel, the Frenchman who inspired anarcho-syndicalism, regarded the workers' revolution as an apocalyptic event, a cleansing of ancient decadence, rather than merely the latest stage in the class struggle. This meant that he idealised 'mass man' and saw in crowd behaviour a modern aesthetic.

Anarcho-syndicalists, including Sorel, attached supreme importance to the power of myth, which they placed above scientific political analysis or rational thought. Myths, Sorel wrote, are neither 'utopias' nor 'descriptions of things'. Instead they are the 'expression of a will', the 'collective consciousness' of the masses in narrative form. Syndicalism's defining myth was the General Strike, through which the workers collectively seize control of the means of production. There was no timetable for this event, nor even a strategy to bring it about. It was, nonetheless, the ultimate goal of anarcho-syndicalist activity, expressed through organisations such as the Confederation General du Travail (CGT) in France[2] and the Industrial Workers of the World (IWW) in the United States. The General Strike was to be an apocalyptic moment, historically and also spiritually: a form of secular Last Judgement. For Sorel, the General Strike myth was an instrument of mass psychology, a means to manipulate those left cold by rationally-based socialist propaganda. It was

> the myth in which all of socialism is contained; that is, it involves a complex of images capable of evoking all the feelings which are raised in the struggle of the socialist movement against contemporary society.[3]

Syndicalism differed from Marxism, and moderate social democracy, in its emphasis on 'evoking feelings' in mass man, rather than appealing to the worker's rational self-interest. A similar stress on 'feeling' above reason became a central component of fascism, and is one of feminist ideology's main tenets as well. Anarcho-syndicalists, in other words, sought to revive the irrational in politics. Unlike Marxists, who regarded themselves as the natural successors to liberals, syndicalists regarded liberal rationalism as a greater enemy than conservative reaction:

> The ferocity of the assault Sorel launched against the liberalism of his own age is thus theoretically as well as practically induced. For it was liberalism that became identified with the stultifying effects of reason and rationalized organization in society.[4]

Anarcho-syndicalism fell out of favour amongst radicals after World War I. The experience of the Great War proved that old patriotic 'myths' were more powerful than modern concoctions such as the General Strike. The Russian Revolution also galvanised a generation of leftists, whilst a new strain of right-wing nationalism combined the appeal to unreason with a propensity for political violence. In its various incarnations, fascism attracted radicals previously drawn to the anarcho-syndicalist tradition. Mussolini himself was born to anarcho-syndicalist parents. His left-wing newspaper, *Avanti*, had been contemptuous of the parliamentary road to socialism, both before and after the War. The 'Corporate State' ideal at the centre of Italian fascism was based on the indirect representation of the individual by members of his profession or social group, rather than direct representation by parliamentarians, an idea adapted from syndicalist trade unions.[5] Germany's National Socialism had, as its name suggests, a collectivist vision of politics. It was a movement led by bohemians and artisans, but competing with left-wing parties for the working class vote. Accordingly, Nazism presented to 'the workers' a distorted version of the class struggle, whereby class became identified with race, the 'greedy capitalist' with the 'profiteering Jew'.

Fascism adapted from syndicalism the idea of the great political myth. In Italy, the myth of the General Strike, through which workers liberated themselves (psychologically and economically) gave way to the myth of the Leader. Because the Leader embodied the people's will, his rule was superior to any form of representative government. The 'Leadership Principle' of the Nazis saw the *Fuhrer* as embodying racial destiny. Whereas anarcho-syndicalists saw irrationalism as a tool of class consciousness, fascists gave mythical status to 'race and nation'. Their conception of nationhood paid no heed to political borders, or to the liberal conception of citizenship conferred regardless of ethnic origin. The nation was based exclusively on racial identity, the political expression of the collective 'folk soul'.

It is easy, too easy, to see fascism as a reactionary movement, because of its racialism and its emphasis on strong leadership. But this is to overlook the radical dynamic of fascist politics, which was driven by hatred of tradition and an obsession with change. Fascist politicians regarded themselves as 'modernisers', working on behalf of 'the people' and asserting the true national interest against a corrupt, conservative and treacherous elite. Their rhetoric of modernisation was more a reflex response than an ideology. Indeed the absence of an ideological goal was interpreted by Hitler as a strength. National Socialism, he claimed, was powered by a 'revolutionary creative will' which had 'no fixed aim' except for the perpetual advancement of the Volk.[6] In contrast to Marxists, who aimed for the 'classless society', National Socialists

> [*knew*] that there is never a final stage, there is no permanency, only eternal change ... the future is an inexhaustible fount of possibilities of further development.[7]

This approach to politics was not as distinct from that of the totalitarian left as Hitler clearly imagined. It had much in common with Trotsky's 'permanent revolution' and the similar doctrines later enunciated by Mao. The shallow rhetoric of modernisation and change bears an uncomfortable resemblance to the slogans of post-socialist politicians in our own time, as they search for an elusive 'third way'.

National Socialism was, therefore, a technocratic movement obsessed with change, which saw the state as the agent of that change and so institutionalised a worship of the state. Yet the irrationalism inherent in fascist movements created an underlying ambivalence about modern society, in particular the alienation of man from the rest of nature. This was not ascribed to urbanisation, technology and the breakdown of traditional authority structures, but to pernicious cultural influence of Semitic origin. Jewish influence 'denatured' German society and diluted German thought. According to Nazi propaganda, the religion of the Jews was 'fossilised' and coldly rational. 'Jewish' reason, 'Jewish' literature, 'Jewish' science and 'Jewish' philosophy had colonised German culture, stifling its creativity. Reconnecting with nature and releasing the Aryan folk soul from bondage meant expunging from German culture all traces of Jewish influence.

Feminist ideology shares National Socialism's ambivalence about modernity and nature. At one level, feminists revere technology and mass society: the former because it encourages women into the work force (and contributes to male unemployment), the latter because it undermines tradition and convention. Yet the demands of feminists are underscored by the idea that 'women', like 'Germans' or 'Aryans' for the Nazis, enjoy a special relationship with the natural world. Thus, as National Socialists blamed 'Jewish money power' for denaturing German society, feminists blame 'male domination' for ecological crisis:

> The patriarchs ... want to continue dominating the Earth, exploiting its forests, minerals and land.[8]

'Men', like 'Jews', have an inferior appreciation of nature. Both groups dominate the economy and culture with a sterile rationalism that suppresses spontaneity and diminishes the importance of the natural world. National Socialism adapted an earlier form of *Volkisch* romanticism, which held that the character of a people could be determined by their natural surroundings, and that the uprooted urban man could connect to his racial 'life force' by exploring mountains and forests:

> Man was seen not as a vanquisher of nature; nor was he credited with the ability to penetrate the meaning of nature by applying the tools of reason; instead he was glorified as living in accordance with nature, at one with its mystical forces. In this way, instead of being encouraged to confront the problems cast up by urbanization and industrialization, man was enticed to retreat into a rural nostalgia. Not within the city, but in the landscape, the countryside native to him, was man fated to merge with and become rooted in nature and the Volk.[9]

From the beginning, this connection between Volk and land-scape was imbued with racist prejudices. The landscape of central Europe, with its mountains, forests and temperate climate, was not considered 'native' to the Jews. They were a 'desert people' whose materialism and rationalism derived from the aridity of their native land. Such notions might seem laughable to the twenty-first century reader, until he realises that feminist academics use the same arguments and the same metaphors, but apply them to men rather than Jews. An American study, *Women's Ways of Knowing*, speaks of male scholars as 'separate knowers', because they emphasise the quest for objective knowledge. 'Separate knowing' is defined as 'the game of impersonal reason', and it has 'traditionally belonged to boys'. Women, by contrast, are 'connected knowers', who respond to feeling and instinct, and for whom sceptical education is inappropriate, since they 'find it easier to believe than to doubt'.[10] Like the proto-Nazi *Volkisch* movement, feminism uses topographical metaphors to exalt and exclude whole categories of humanity. For feminists, however, mountains are evil and patriarchal, the strongholds of male 'vertical thinking'. Valleys, by contrast, are lush, fertile and feminine, the source of 'lateral thinking'. Dr Peggy McIntosh, an educational theorist in Massachusetts who helps design high school curricula, questions the need for schools to focus on the 'mountain strongholds of white men' and calls for a shift to 'valley values' – the intuitional approach of women, and also she claims of 'ethnic minorities'[11]. In the same way that National Socialism diverted environmental consciousness towards racial hatred, feminism exploits 'green' issues to further its hatred of masculinity. This has created a form of man-hating green politics known as ecofeminism.[12] Where Nazis argued that 'Aryans' were closer to nature than Jews, ecofeminists contend that women are closer to nature than men. For humanity and nature to reunite, instinctual female values must triumph over male reason:

> [T]o the extent that women's lives have been lived in ways which are less directly oppositional to nature than those of men, and have involved different and less oppositional practices, qualities of care and kinds of selfhood, an ecological feminist position could and should privilege some to the experiences and practices of women over those of men ...[13]

In its attack on 'male' reason, 'male philosophy', 'male science' and 'hegemonic, phallocentric literature'[14], this brand of green feminism echoes uncannily the Nazi attack on Jewish 'hegemony'. As part of its appeal to unreason, Nazi ideology made use, selectively, of the pre-Christian faith of Northern Europe, distorting heroic legends to justify racial triumphalism.[15] Ecofeminists similarly attempt to revive the cult of the 'Indo-European' Earth Goddess, through a series of selective and vague references which omit such uncomfortable details as human sacrifice. This bowdlerised paganism is part of a larger attempt to deconstruct, and de-rationalise, Western culture, to cleanse it of male influence which represses affinity with nature. Hazel Henderson, a prominent ecofeminist, speaks of 'the neurotic notion of scientific objectivity' as the product of centuries of alleged male supremacy:

> We see it in the long saga of patriarchal literature, from the Greek myths of the hero and the hero's journey to the angst and alienation from Nature echoed from Hegel, Marx and the Frankfurt School to Hermann Hesse, the existentialists, Sigmund Freud and his followers.[16]

The rhetoric of philistinism and cultural destructiveness is familiar to anyone who has lived under an extreme right-wing regime. Yet the targets of Henderson's anger are most significant. Objectivity, for example, ensures the freedom of the individual under the rule of law. It guarantees that academic study, whether artistic or scientific, is based on dispassionate inquiry rather than crude propaganda. To ecofeminists and National Socialists, however, the quest for objectivity is respectively a male and Jewish evil. Likewise the hero's journey, in the Western tradition, is not about male 'domination' at all, but the ways by which a man acquires compassion, wisdom and a feeling for his fellow creatures. True compassion has nothing to do with ecofeminist values, which place collective consciousness above individual wisdom and sentimentality above knowledge. Significantly, too, the male thinkers Henderson attacks were ridiculed by the Nazis in identical terms: many were persecuted or exiled by the National Socialist regime. Henderson's replacement for 'patriarchal' Western culture is a 'feminised' irrationalism based (like the Aryan 'folk culture' of the Third Reich) on biased pseudo-history linked to a simplistic variant of 'New Age' pantheism:

> Women's spirituality affirms and celebrates human embeddedness in Nature, and confirms it by researching [sic] the early matrifocal cultures and humanity's first great universal religion: that of the Great Mother Goddess.

Today's eco-feminism is restoring this earlier prehistory, its art and rituals celebrating Nature. Eco-feminism re-sacralises Nature.[17]

With an uncanny resemblance to National Socialist and Volksich thinkers, Henderson brushes aside the practical dilemmas thrown up by the rejection of rational culture. She does not, for instance, express an intention to stop taking 'male' medicine or disconnect her drains because they were designed and installed by male engineers. Many of her conclusions amount to incitement to hatred against men in general, male scientists and creators in particular. She also speaks of a 'Solar Age' and of emerging 'through today's crises and clouds into the sunshine of an Age of Light'.[18] Sun worship, and the 'symbolism of the reborn sun'[19] were beloved of National Socialists as well. Nazi racial theorist Johann von Leers, author of an anti-Semitic tract called 'Jews, Look At You' believed that Nordic peoples had a special relationship with the sun, and that through Nazism they were emerging from 'fog' into 'light'.[20] His attitude towards 'objectivity' and 'reason' looks similar to Henderson's, except that the hate targets are Semitic rather than male. Henderson becomes interesting, however, when she explains in pseudo-scientific terms the ecofeminist view of the individual:

> I believe there is a deeper layer underlying the old issue of the individual versus the state, ... Perhaps the deeper and biologically irreconcilable conflict is that of the individual human phenotype versus the species genotype. ... Only a statistically insignificant number of phenotypes ever produces a genetically useful innovation of form or function that survives and is incorporated into the human gene pool. From the perspective of the genotype (the species as a whole) the fate of each individual phenotype is irrelevant.[21]

When we transcend the jargon, we find that the individual human being – the 'phenotype' – has no inherent value and is 'relevant' only as part of a larger group, the 'genotype'. Even within that group, his significance is peripheral and linked only to his ability to produce a 'genetically useful innovation'. In Henderson's ecofeminist schema, the relationship between 'phenotype' and 'genotype' matches the National Socialist conception of the individual's relationship with the Volk. Under both systems, feminist and Nazi, the individual is deprived of political freedom and personal autonomy[22]. His thoughts, feelings, needs and values count for nothing against the collective will.

Both systems also favour eugenics. Henderson, and other ecofeminists, are fanatical devotees of 'population control', whilst National Socialists favoured selective breeding and its inevitable corollary, selective sterilisation. With equal inevitability, the 'old issue of the individual versus the state' is resolved decisively in favour of the latter.[23] For the all-powerful state expresses the underlying will of the Volk or interprets the underlying 'rhythms' of the genotype. National Socialists identify the state with 'race and nation', the nation forcibly enlarged to include all members of the 'race', whether they wish to be included or not. Ecofeminists envisage the state as a creche on a gigantic scale, a world-wide matriarchal tyranny. These two ideas of the state might seem opposed to each other, but they are essentially the same. This is because they both call for the dissolution of political borders between nations, shaped by historical events and confirmed by democratic consent. They both reject the concept of the individual that has been central to Western thought since classical antiquity, reaffirmed by the Judaeo-Christian tradition and by liberal political thought. That is to say, the individual as a being who is capable of moral choice, who has an inherent value, a right to life and a responsibility to himself and others.[24] And last, but by no means least, both the National Socialist and ecofeminist world views are founded on hatred and exclusion. Their opponents – Jews and male homosexuals for the Nazis, males of whatever type for the ecofeminists – are less close to nature and so it follows that they must also be less human.[25]

Feminist ideology and its fascist precursor take the impulses behind orthodox socialism and transfer them towards alternative goals. The idea of collective consciousness is shifted from 'class' towards allegiances of 'race' or 'gender'. Collective hatred for the 'ruling class' is shifted towards 'male supremacy', 'Jewish money power', 'sexist philosophy' or 'degenerate art'. Feminism resembles fascism in that it combines a contempt for the individual and hatred of tradition, inherited from the revolutionary left, with mystical irrationalism and sentimentality. The popularity of feminist clichés amongst Western 'progressives' testifies to the intellectual impoverishment and paralysis of will on the left. From the 1970s onwards, feminism's rise correlates with a reduction of interest in the 'good society' for all citizens. The purpose of progressive politics is ceasing to the betterment of the condition of the whole people, or creating a sense of community that transcends economic and social divisions. It is now less about affording opportunities to individuals, more about refashioning society into a series of abstract patterns.

One of feminism's most striking features is its contempt, even hatred, for its supposed constituents, namely women themselves. It is a characteristic shared with other totalitarian ideologies. Marxism constantly berated the working class for its 'false consciousness', susceptibility to bourgeois propaganda, reformism and individualism. Fascist leaders similarly exhorted members of 'their' race and nation to live up to a twisted ideal of greatness. Under Marxist regimes, workers who challenged authority, or retained traditional beliefs, were deemed 'class traitors' and dealt with by summary injustice. National Socialism often persecuted its 'Aryan' critics as if they were Jews. Hermann Hesse, who is condemned by Henderson on feminist grounds, was forced in to exile by the Third Reich. His books, which reflect a concern for nature more profound than that of any Nazi or feminist, were banned by Hitler's regime. This phenomenon of self-appointed group leaders excoriating members of 'their' groups is repeated, with gusto, in single issue campaigns of modern times.

Both in its ecofeminist and unisexist guises, feminism is unremittingly hostile to real women. Ecofeminism recycles, as articles of feminist faith, the very arguments that were once deployed against women's advancement in politics and the professions. Women are intuitive rather than rational, feeling rather than thinking, subjective rather than dispassionate. They have an abstract connection with 'nature' that is not shared by men, and which is more important than their relationships with male lovers, husbands and sons. It is a very great insult to the rational woman to tell her that reason is 'male', that the Western cultural tradition is 'patriarchal' and so not for her, and that her capacity for reason is somehow incompatible with her natural feelings of love or concern.[26] Equally, it is insulting to the rational man to tell him that he is disconnected from nature, inherently violent (towards 'women' and 'nature' alike) and incapable of thinking about, let alone solving, environmental problems. Ecofeminism misunderstands the entire basis of political ecology, because it is using 'nature' only as a weapon of war. The origins of ecological concern do not lie in a conflict between male and female principles, but in men and women thinking rationally about the economy and society, then questioning the assumptions of both. Unease about the effects of unlimited economic growth on the environment, or the moral effects of unbridled consumerism, is rooted in reasoned thought and confirmed by objective inquiry.

Ecofeminism ignores real women, as individuals, and substitutes an idealised vision of Woman, connected mystically to nature but divided irrevocably from Man. Unisexism, meanwhile, dismisses femininity, like masculinity, as a 'social construct', seeks to abolish female as well as male spheres of influence, to abolish the delicacy that surrounds relations between the sexes, indeed all intimate relationships, and replace it with a matter-of-fact promiscuity. In seeking to erase all differences between male and female, unisex feminism undermines the values of kindness and respect for private space that enable men and women to treat each other with dignity.

Unisexists demand the overthrow of masculine values, the abolition of 'male' institutions and the use of 'educational' brainwashing to abolish differences between the sexes.[27] Yet the 'traditional' woman, who is well-disposed towards men, dislikes female 'role models' in business or politics and is disgusted by the thought of women being sent to the front line is considered as much a thought criminal as the 'traditional' man who believes in the male role of protector and provider. In place of the masculine, the unisexist vision offers not femininity, but androgyny. Feminists today often openly celebrate the androgynous. Henderson, for example, speaks of the 'rising, ecologically-aware androgynized concern for the future', proving that ecofeminism and unisexism do not contradict each other, but are part of the same ideological attack on individual freedom.[28] Attempts to impose 'androgynous' values are, in practice, coarsening and demoralising to members of both sexes. Often, they have the very opposite effect to the desired end. In his masterly study of the demoralising effects of 'feminisation' on the American military, Brian Mitchell cites a study of male cadets at the US Air Force Academy in 1980, the year they were 'integrated' with women:

> Wilson and Gillman [concluded] that the few experiences actually shared by both male and female cadets served to diminish rather than increase the attachment of males to the academy and to their class, particularly to their female classmates. Though shared experiences do serve to bond men together when "the major social value of military society is a warrior image", at the Air Force Academy "a new social value of an androgynous warrior was pressed upon the members of the institution".

The sharing of experience by men and women in order to mold androgynous warriors would necessarily have made the women more masculine and the men more feminine, had not the men resisted this imposi-
tion on their inner self. Instead of growing closer, male and female cadets
grew further apart.[29]

The rite of passage for young people is one of the constants of
human societies, 'developed' or otherwise. At times, it involves the
separation of the sexes, so that their distinctive needs can be
addressed. Yet that separation is balanced, creatively, by interaction
between them. The balance is not easy to strike, and some societies
over-emphasise sexual segregation, for youth and adults alike.
Feminism's mistake is to confuse all single-sex activities with
inequality, to assume that the removal of barriers to success for
women means that the existence of male and female spheres of influence must always be wrong. Unisexists fail to recognise that single-
sex activities, and institutions, need not be oppressive. Instead, they
can help preserve that social balance which affords to both men and
women greater freedom. The unisexist attack on 'male' institutions,
from the Armed Forces to the 'patriarchal family' is contributing to
unhappiness, alienation and violence amongst young men – violence
directed against themselves and others, including women. Rather
than address these questions, unisexism advocates such emotional
cul-de-sacs as 'political lesbianism' and demands the 'right' of
women to raise children without men. So grievous are the consequences of these feminist approaches to individual freedom, social
stability and the welfare of children that women themselves are
leading the revolt against the new dogmas.

Ecofeminism, therefore, contributes to the unisexist canon and
gives it ersatz 'green' credentials. Both approaches are founded on
hatred for half of the human race, and for the very culture that
permits free expression of their ideas. They are part of an ideology
that places abstract concepts of 'gender' before individual affections
and preferences. This cold-hearted collectivism contains in it the
seeds of its own destruction. For the experience of twentieth century
totalitarianism offers two lessons. The first is that placing the group
before the individual produces only suffering. The second is that
using the state to alter human nature ends only in human catastrophe.

8. Afterword: Beyond Liberal Fundamentalism

Much of the discussion in these chapters has been about the paradoxes of modern liberalism. Chief amongst these are inequality in the name of equality, state control in the name of freedom, censorship in the name of 'tolerance', 'gender' quotas in the name of 'opportunity for all' and, to combat racism, an almost pathological emphasis on race. But however paradoxical, however contradictory and however unworkable in practice these ideological tenets might be, they remain articles of new liberal faith, absorbed and largely unquestioned even by some of the new liberalism's fiercest critics.

The surrender of 'old' liberalism, as we have seen, is more or less complete; it offers only token concessions to differences between individuals and occasional nervous pleas on behalf of benign traditions, such as freedom of speech. Socialists, who are embattled in the economic sphere, tend to accept the cultural premises of new liberalism, instead of acknowledging its role in perpetuating economic privilege, competition for its own sake and a materialistic consumer culture. Greens, anarchists and the burgeoning 'anti-globalisation' movement[1] would, one might have thought, be natural critics of political correctness. It is, after all, the most globalising of ideologies, universalist in its assumptions, missionary in its campaigning zeal[2] and highly authoritarian in its approach to the role of government.

Green politics, by contrast, should be at least as much conservative as it is radical. The desire to preserve natural diversity might be expected to accompany a commitment to human diversity, whilst concern for long-established ecosystems and concern for traditional cultures should go together as love and marriage did in musical romances long ago. Some pioneers of the green movement, like Edward Goldsmith, have made a consistent connection between ecology and culture, between conserving what was best, and most carefully evolved, in human societies and conserving natural habitats.³ However the prevailing tone of eco-politics in the United States and Western Europe is one of unequivocal support for the new liberal agenda and the promotion of group rights above both individual freedom and traditional restraints. The concept of 'living within limits' does not extend to the demand for 'rights' by pressure groups, whose scope is perceived to be limitless and whose demands are grafted incongruously onto many a green agenda.

Anarchism has also seen an unprecedented, but not altogether surprising, revival since the end of the Cold War and the crisis of socialist thought. For it is, after all, untainted by memories of oppression and bloodshed. Despite the sporadic use of terrorism by anarchists, there is also in their thinking a strong pacifist and mystical strain, reflected in the 'civil disobedience' of Henry David Thoreau, for example, that influenced Gandhi and later Martin Luther King. Unlike Marxism, but like certain forms of liberalism, anarchist thought is informed by a strong sense of the individual, or at least a balance between the individual and the collective. And, like the green movement, anarchist thinkers favour community over bureaucracy, ethical codes over written charters, human scale economics over large units of production, whether they are controlled by corporate business or the state.⁴ It is, as one critic describes, a 'feeling that all organisation, whether revolutionary or repressive, socialist or capitalist, [is] bad, and that if only men could be freed from it altogether they would live happily in peace with each other'.⁵ Most importantly, perhaps, it is also untried, except in parts of Spain during the 1930s, where anarchist militias imposed a regime of genuine egalitarianism combined with Puritan austerity.

Historically more popular amongst artisans, craftsmen and itinerant labourers, as opposed to industrial workers and students, anarchism has a conservative strand not shared by other revolutionary movements. Proudhon, who is regarded as the modern movement's founder, was explicitly socially conservative, even reactionary. Both he, and the influential Russian thinker Peter Kropotkin, idealised the peasant commune, with its emphasis on a sense of place. Yet the modern anarchist revival is characterised by a sweeping universalism, its activists allying themselves with the far left as stormtroopers for politically correct campaigns.⁶ The anti-globalisation protesters have come closest in recent years to creating a large-scale social movement not linked to 'identity politics'. Nonetheless, they have tended so far to be reactive in their approach. They place coalition building before both the theory and practice of politics, defining themselves by what they are against rather than what they are 'for'. The idea that globalisation and political correctness are two sides of the same coin has not occurred to many of them. To others it is potentially divisive, or represents a positive threat to their 'left-wing' worldview. Indeed some of the most strident opponents of economic globalisation are the strongest champions of global political correctness, whilst some of the strongest opponents of 'monopoly capitalism' and multinationals favour the stringent regulation of small business.[7] Far from advocating as much variety in human affairs as possible, they favour forms of 'global governance' that involve imposing Western, new liberal norms whether they are wanted or not. They scorn local customs and personal choice with the zeal of new liberal activists and legislators – and the corporations they oppose, which are often rigidly politically correct and use new liberal nostrums as instruments of control.[8]

Conservatives, equally, are muted in their criticisms of political correctness. Their response varies from intemperate outbursts that lack coherence, to a timid and at times abject intellectual surrender. Superficially examined, this approach calls to mind Evelyn Waugh's rebuke to the Conservative Party that it had not put the clock back one second in half a century. Waugh was of course wrong, because the purpose of conservatism has been to manage change rather than putting back the clock, to build on traditions rather than erase them or preserve them in aspic. To paraphrase Burke, the thoughtful conservative seeks 'to improve on what we already know', instead of destroying and then attempting to rebuild, like the revolutionary Jacobins. It is therefore in managing change, rather than putting the clock back, that modern conservatism is failing. The increasing surrender of conservatives to politically correct assumptions about group rights should not be seen as a simple loss of nerve. Instead, it is complementary to an earlier surrender, in which social stability and continuity were sacrificed to the dogma of market forces, so that an asocial libertarianism on the right competed with collectivist group rights on the left.

Today's conservative 'modernisers', on both ides of the Atlantic, are ahead of the green left in seeing the connection between political correctness and market fundamentalism. They see this link as desirable, interpreting political correctness as a form of 'social liberalism' to complement the economic liberalism of the unfettered market. There is a sense in which they are quite right. The new social liberalism, after all, speaks of diversity and inclusion, co-opting the rhetoric of civil liberties, but it quickly hardens into a an authoritarian pseudo-liberalism because it takes too little account of the way real people think and feel. In this, it matches well the doctrine of market supremacy, which is as rigid and inflexible as the state socialist dogma it has supplanted. Economic liberalism is a largely unreconstructed nineteenth century ideology that views the individual as a unit of production and consumption rather than a living, breathing being. In this sense, it resembles the form of vulgar Marxism that has influenced the growth of identity politics. Unlike Marx at his best, this sub-Marxist approach allows no room for individual men or women, seeing them only in terms of group identity, much as 'neo-liberal' economists cannot envisage them except in materialistic terms as producers and consumers.

The sub-Marxist vision of politics, so compatible in practice with consumer-capitalism of the most crass kind, is found amongst Trotskyist groups rather than orthodox Communists. It is linked to a belief in 'permanent' revolution, an imperative of continuous change that is shared by market fundamentalists, who abhor traditional restraint. The New Left of the 1960s drew much inspiration from Trotskyism, because it was seen as an unsullied alternative to the hated Soviet model, less exotic – and requiring less discipline – than Maoism. Trotskyist groups survived the Cold War for similar reasons. They see in identity politics a 'revolutionary potential' and see themselves as the vanguard of politically correct campaigns.[9] Free-market fundamentalism also aims at permanent revolution, and the casting off of institutional and ethical restraints that inhibit the free play of economic forces.

In its attacks on tradition, its zealous secularism and its quest for 'level playing field' uniformity[10], the economic agendas of market fundamentalism mirror the political agendas of the new 'social liberalism'. Much as new liberals divide the population arbitrarily into groups, without reference to the way people really identify themselves, market fundamentalists see 'marketing niches' before real nations, real communities and real people. New liberalism, in practice, creates authoritarian bureaucracies obsessed with 'discrimination', rather than the free society its advocates claim to want. Market fundamentalism stifles the competition and variety it claims to foster, because it permits the rise of private, corporate monopolies as restrictive of choice as the worst of all nationalised concerns. Under the reign of market forces, small businesses and family farms go to the wall, manufacturing regions are impoverished and insecurity becomes a permanent feature of working life. Despite their professed rationalism, radical free marketers are curiously superstitious, professing blind faith in a 'Hidden Hand' that guides all things.

Market fundamentalism shares with political correctness an abhorrence of national or cultural boundaries and the varied laws and practices they encompass. Supporters of both, therefore, have a shared interest in promoting political and cultural uniformity, and the institutions that promote it. They assume, like the 'littérateurs' of pre-Revolutionary France, that a common framework can be found into which all human beings can be slotted and that once this 'system' is imposed, we shall all react in predictable ways. The new social liberals and the 'neo-liberal' partisans of market forces both believe that cultural differences between nations and peoples are irrelevant, even if they have evolved over centuries or millennia, and that humanity can be refashioned to fit crude economic or group-based stereotypes. The market fundamentalist, for example, has a vested interest in seeing the goals of gender feminism realised, so that men and women are indistinguishable from each other as units of production and both conform to a corporate world view, in which they are socially interchangeable economic competitors. Furthermore, like the abolition of nationhood, the abolition of family structures, along with the assumptions and commitments underlying them, reduces the individual to a purely economic status: *homo economicus*, as an earlier generation of free market radicals put it.

Market fundamentalists, therefore, seek to remove all barriers between the individual and the market. In the name of political correctness, meanwhile, new liberals wish to remove all barriers between the individual and the state. These two goals are not at all far removed from each other. For there is already a symbiotic relationship between large political units, especially those which transcend national frontiers or suppress regional cultures, and transnational corporations which believe that their form of wealth creation is valid for all human beings, all cultures and all ecosystems.

A breakdown of civil society is occasioned both by social engi-neering that undermines family and community, and by free-market doctrines that undermine our sense of shared citizenship and respon-sibility to each other. This breakdown increases the role of the state in controlling the lives of individuals, mediating between them, defining their 'rights' and holding their rebellious impulses in check. Market fundamentalists require, in practice, a strong state to prevent popular revolt against economic policies that enrich some but impoverish others and create an atmosphere of continuous anxiety for rich and poor alike. One of the main features of free-market ideology in the modern epoch is that its application has a 'proletarianising' effect on the middle-class. This is because the sense of obligation (economic or moral) between employer and employee is increasingly dissolved, whilst the creative energies and aptitudes of many professionals and skilled workers, especially older males, who are both expensive and politically incorrect to employ. It is only through the recourse to repression that dissent can be effectively contained and the behaviour of an increasingly restless, fragmented population modified.

Politically correct activists are similarly quite willing to use force, especially against those who are economically and socially powerless, to secure power for themselves as well as advancing their sectional interests. The 'anti-racist' movement in Britain is a case in point, as it is for the most part a coalition of bureaucrats and comfortably-off activists, practising an inverted class struggle against indigenous com-munities, with no impact on the welfare of black people or other ethnic groups.[11] Anti-racist campaigners, who are overwhelmingly white, tend when they encounter a black man to see him more as a social issue and less as a human being. They also seek quite conscious-ly to perpetuate racial divisions and draw attention to differences of race, in order to block the development of a civic consciousness that transcends ethnicity and makes the race relations industry redundant. In his admirable study of the future of England and 'Englishness', the former MP Sir Richard Body describes an illuminating incident, in which an official, acting out anti-racist ideological precepts, tries to destroy a situation of racial harmony:

> In writing this book I heard many examples of ... attempts to create racial consciousness where it did not exist before. On one occasion, a youth club in the East End was visited by an official from the borough council who had every appearance of being on the militant Left. He

asked to meet "the chair". When he heard of this, the chairman said he did not believe in "furniturism", which may not have got the conversation off to a good start. It continued as follows:

The official: "I have come about the council's grant. I have to explain that its renewal depends upon the proportion of ethnic minorities in the club."

The chairman: "I simply don't know about them."

The official: "Then how many black members are recorded?"

The chairman: "That is something we would never think of recording. This is a club and open to any youngster who likes to join and accepts the rules. I don't care a damn about their colour; it has got nothing to do with their membership."

The official: "You can't receive a grant unless you record their ethnic origin, so that we can see from your books you are carrying out the council's policy."

The chairman, disturbed by the line of conversation, called in the club's leader, a young man, black and of Jamaican origin.

Chairman: "I have no idea." A pause. "I think there may be many more blacks than whites."

Official: "In that case you will be entitled to a renewal of the council's grant if you can prove it, but you must record the figures for inspection."

Chairman: "We will do no such thing. That is blatant racialism. You can keep the grant. I would rather find the money myself, and I will, rather than agree to this talk about race."

The Club leader nodded his total support and the official went his way

How does the multiculturalist answer this obvious question: Who has done more to create racial harmony in this corner of England? Is it the club leader in his numerous activities, social and sporting, that bring young people together, or is it the council official with his bribe to goad black youngsters to think of their racial difference?[12]

Sir Richard called his book *England for the English*. A question mark after that title might have expressed its meaning more clearly, since the book raises questions about the prsent and future, rather than reiterating past certainties. However the underlying theme of the book is to achieve a genuinely inclusive definition of English identity[13], as distinct from the ersatz 'inclusivity' of multiculturalism, which draws attention to racial differences and is not even, in practice, very culturally tolerant.[14] The answer to his question above is obvious enough – the club leader and chairman. The ideology of the official is unconcerned with an inclusive definition of Englishness, or even of an inclusive local identity. It is concerned instead with one-size-fits-all solutions that increase the power of the state and take power away from civil society.

The theory underlying free-market fundamentalism was that it would roll back the frontiers of the state. In practice, it has reduced the influence of civil society and so increased the influence of movements that balkanise the population, both within nations and on a global scale. One of the paradoxes of globalisation, and the ideology behind it, is that instead of being a unifying force, it creates a more fragmented world. The rise of violent forms of identity politics in Asia and Africa, and less violent, but profoundly intolerant forms in the supposedly 'developed' world, is part and parcel of the globalising process, not a reaction against it:

> In *Jihad vs. McWorld*, Benjamin Barber represented the 'new' capitalism as a form of 'economic totalism' (*McWorld*), locked into a dialectical relationship with the 'tribalism' that its universalising tendencies provoked. *Jihad* was a metaphor for this 'tribalism', an identity politics turned cancerous, which Barber saw crystallising around the globe in response to the relentless advance of *McWorld*. Both *Jihad* and *McWorld* gnawed away at the foundations of democracy, and unless an alternative to the struggle between the two could be found, the epoch on whose threshold we stood – 'postcommunist, postindustrial, postnational, yet sectarian, fearful and bigoted' – was 'likely also to be terminally postdemocratic'.[15]

Those varieties of Third World identity politics grouped conveniently together under the title 'Jihad' have much in common with those movements in the West that I have conveniently grouped together as 'political correctness'. The methods might be very different, but the underlying principles are almost identical: the group instead of the individual, the abolition of tradition, the state or the corporation in place of civil society. Both 'Jihad'-based fundamentalist and politically correct campaigns combine a sense of historical destiny or inevitability with a missionary impulse to impose their will on others.

Thus Islamic fundamentalism is merely the most fearsome expression to date of a worldwide upsurge in militant identity politics. Identity-based movements place collective loyalties before individual freedom, offer simplistic explanations for complex problems and demonise their opponents as enemies or traitors. Far from being 'reactionary', or even conservative, they all display a radical disdain for history, tradition and continuity. Rather than aiming to turn the clock back, as Waugh would have wished, or to manage change constructively, as a more thoughtful conservative would hope, they seek to impose their multifarious visions of Utopia.

The ideology of radical Islamists, such as the former Taliban regime in Afghanistan – a student movement originally, like the New Left[16] – has more in common with the secular totalitarianisms of the twentieth century than it does with traditional Islam, with its scholarship, rational scientific inquiry, legalism and philosophical speculation. Islamic fundamentalism distorts the beliefs and customs of the Muslim world, much as the Nazis temporarily distorted German culture for their own purposes and racists today distort the concept of nationhood. Indeed, like 'National Socialism' – and, in a different sense, like Communism or Pan-Europeanism – Islamic fundamentalism looks beyond the nation-state, placing religious faith above national or local cultures much as the *Volkisch* movement placed race before any other considerations, or the left, at its most simplistic, placed class.[17] Significantly, the motif of the British National Party, the most prominent 'far right' movement in the United Kingdom, is 'Rights for Whites', a conscious echo of the slogans of politically correct campaigns. Similar movements in continental Europe and the United States adopt the same rhetoric. Theirs is, after all, a political correctness of the right.

Other fundamentalisms do not, for the most part, practise terrorism; their intimidation, when it occurs, is subtler, ranging from emotional blackmail through censorious legislation to simplistic and ritually repeated slogans that polarise opinion. The 'Religious Right', in American politics especially, invokes Christ's teachings and claims to be defending liberty. However its spokesmen show scant respect for the liberties of their opponents, denigrate other faiths and are singularly lacking in either compassion or forgiveness. Ironically, the Christian right in its fanaticism has reverted to the Pharisaic obsession with laws, structures and regulations applied in a rigid manner that allows no room for individual need or specific circumstances. This is a trait it shares with other types of fundamentalism, which adopt a Procrustean approach to the individual, forcing him to fit into theoretical constructs such as 'the class system' or the 'gender system', whether or not they express his best interests, needs or even simple wishes. Gender feminism is also a fundamentalist movement that has little interest in the needs of 'real' women, but plenty of theories about 'what women want' or ought to want. This is why gender feminists vilify women who oppose them, along with a male 'enemy' that includes boys as well as men.[18] The gay rights movement also promotes a fundamentalist ideology and, as already noted, has rituals and vocabulary that seem consciously to mirror those of evangelical Protestantism. The process of 'coming out' has much in common with being 'born again' in evangelical parlance, whilst the 'lesbian and gay societies' in universities are pious, stubbornly asexual gatherings that resemble Christian Union meetings more closely than any other aspect of campus life.[19] Like religious funda-mentalists, gay activists believe that there is only one path to salva-tion or 'liberation' – theirs – and that their special insights justify the use of force, for example the 'outing' of their opponents.[20]

This book has identified a number of closely overlapping ten-dencies, described them variously as new liberalism, pseudo-liberal-ism and identity politics, or used the popular catch-all term political correctness. Ultimately, it might be more useful to see political cor-rectness as a form of liberal fundamentalism. Common to all funda-mentalisms is a distortion of noble or worthy ideals into extreme and twisted ideological fanaticism. Political correctness distorts the original principles of liberalism at several levels. First, it takes as its starting point the liberal idea that society can be perpetually improved, using this premise as an excuse for social engineering, the attempt to transform human nature (which is assumed to be infi-nitely malleable) and an indiscriminate attack on traditions and customs. The liberal belief in the individual, who has responsibilities as well as rights, is turned into a belief in groups, to which individu-als automatically belong, their problems solved collectively rather than on an individual or personal basis. Thus the idea of civil society, transcending differences such as race, class or sex, gives way to a society divided precisely along these lines, in which 'identity' groups are represented by activists, with the state acting as mediator between collective claims instead of being the upholder of personal liberty. The liberal demand that women should have the chance to participate fully as citizens, contributing to economic and political life, gives way to an ideological attack on masculinity and femininity alike. The belief that nations should co-operate gives way to a soulless internationalism, which scorns any sense of place or loyalty to the nation-state and favours impersonal, bureaucratic blocs of standardised political ideology and identical economic systems.

Liberal fundamentalists continue to expropriate the language of traditional liberalism. They speak in terms of civil liberties and 'human rights'. They make frequent appeal to individual liberty, although they rarely if ever distinguish it from group rights, or distinguish individual need from group identity, except to create subgroups ('women of colour'; 'black lesbians', etc.). The co-option of liberal vocabulary by politically correct partisans is not, in the strict sense, a deception. Most traditional liberals have been less than energetic in defence of individual freedom and civil society, with the result that there is little in the way of a 'progressive' alternative to the politically correct campaigns. Conservative – and socialist – criticism of political correctness is muted for two reasons. First, there is the inherent difficulty in providing a comprehensive enough critique of liberal fundamentalism that is still both pragmatic and humane. This is because opponents of this way of looking at the world tend to be instinctively distrustful of theories, systems and grand designs. They dislike the dictates of political correctness because they regard them as dehumanising to the point of absurdity. Rather than criticise systematically, which might require a 'totalistic' approach uncomfortably similar to political correctness itself, they react with mild satire or a benign shrug of the shoulders, a healthy yet insufficient response to fanaticism.

The second difficulty is that many of the goals of politically correct movements appear compatible with a decent society and seem to address genuine injustices, past and present. Those who are made anxious by the ascendancy of global capitalism, and seek a more human alternative, are likely to attach themselves to any political tendency that might point tentatively toward social justice and a more equitable world order. In so doing, they tend to overlook the flaws in such movements, on the grounds that they are the best 'on offer'. In practice, this is little more than clutching at straws. Liberal fundamentalism is not a rival to market fundamentalism, but gives globalisation a cultural underpinning. The ethics of fairness and social responsibility deserve a better political vehicle.

It is quite easy, then, to see why so many of our well-meaning and politically articulate citizens give in to liberal fundamentalism, despite their misgivings. But there is an alternative approach. George Orwell, a socialist also a liberal in the true sense of the word, reflected on aspects of the English character that inoculate against totalitarian impulses:

> But here it is worth noting a minor English trait which is extremely well marked though not often commented on, and that is a love of flowers. This is one of the first things that one notices when one reaches England from abroad, especially if one is coming from southern Europe. Does it not contradict the English indifference to the arts? Not really, because it is found in people who have no aesthetic feeling whatever. What it does link up with, however, is another English characteristic which is so much a part of us that we barely notice it, and that is the addiction to hobbies and spare-time occupations, the *privateness* of English life. We are a nation of flower lovers, but also a nation of stamp-collectors, pigeon-fanciers, amateur carpenters, coupon-snippers, darts-players, cross-word-puzzle fans. All the culture that is most truly native centres round things which even when communal are not official – the pub, the football match, the back garden, the fireside and the 'nice cup of tea'. The liberty of the individual is still believed in, almost as in the nineteenth century. But this has nothing to do with economic liberty, the right to exploit others for profit. It is the liberty to have a home of your own, to do what you like in your spare time, to choose your own amusements instead of having them chosen for you from above. The most hateful of all names in an English ear is Nosey Parker. It is obvious, of course, that even this purely private liberty is a lost cause. Like all other modern people, the English are in the process of being numbered, labelled, con-scripted, 'co-ordinated'. But the pull of their impulses is in the other direction, and the kind of regimentation that can be imposed on them will be modified in consequence. No party rallies, no Youth Movements, no coloured shirts, no Jew-baiting or ' spontaneous' demonstrations. No Gestapo either, in all probability.[21]

Such characteristics are not unique to England, but they have been peculiarly effective guards against fashionable 'isms'. Orwell's patriotic sentiments and opposition to an elitist vanguard of intellectuals made him unfashionable on the left in 1940, when he wrote the above words. It was an era when rival totalitarian ideologies confronted – and sometimes collaborated with – each other on the European stage and when the left-wing intelligentsia evaded the truth about Soviet Communism. Amongst metropolitan liberals, it could be said that sympathy with the Soviet Union was as commonplace as support for political correct causes today. Orwell, however, was referring to a British, and perhaps especially an English tradition of tolerance, transcending boundaries of 'left' and 'right'.

This ethos of tolerance is founded on a resistance to the idea that every aspect of life is political, or can be politicised. It is based on freedom of association and an acknowledgement that individuals have different interests and needs, and so the attempt to impose a 'one-size-fits-all' equality will surely fail, and surely create greater iniquity. It is anti-bureaucratic and based on devolution of power downwards – to local communities and self-governing nations, not those faceless power blocs that Orwell satirised to such effect in *1984*. Such an approach to politics and society is quite different from the politically correct view of the world, which sanctions limitless bureaucratic interference and 'harmonisation' of all aspects of life, placing equality before freedom to the eventual detriment of both.

Orwell was right to fear the trends towards regimentation and numbering as politicians became increasingly in thrall to ideological fashion and the endless pursuit of 'progress'. If we are to resist such trends, at home and abroad, we must cast off the simplistic slogans of group rights and seek a politics that reflects the complexities of human life. This takes courage, because it is easier to take refuge in slogans or find safety in a conformist crowd. Yet if we value freedom, and fairness, then this is precisely what we must do.

Notes

Preface

1   John Green, London W5, 'Letter of the Week', *New Statesman*, 14 January 2002.

Chapter 1

1   Jeff was unable to tell me which countries had passed such laws, referring to Scandinavia as if it were one country.

2   For a more detailed account of the formation and roles of these societies, see James R. Walker *Lakota Belief and Ritual* (Edited by Raymond J. DeMallie and Elaine A. Jahner; Lincoln and London: University of Nebraska Press, 1990).

3   In this case, presumably by amending the Sex Discrimination Act (1974) to remove the exemption applying to private clubs. It is believed that some members of the Labour administration of 1997-2001 contemplated such moves, but that they were abandoned, ironically because of their human rights implications.

4   Over thirty US states still officially outlaw homosexual 'sodomy'. In the 1986 Bowers vs. Hardwick case, the Supreme Court found in favour of the State of Georgia and upheld the 'constitutionality' of such laws.

5   Richard Clutterbuck, *Protest and the Urban Guerrilla* (London: Cassell, 1973), pp.147-8

6   Clutterbuck, cites a pamphlet by the 'libertarian' left group Solidarity in the early 1970s called 'Strategy for Industrial Struggle'. This includes a practical guide to industrial sabotage. An example cited approvingly is Italy, where 'Alfa Romeo produced 10,000 fewer cars than its planned programme, with losses which could hit its whole ambitious expansion programme in the impoverished South'. '*The net effect of this* [Clutterbuck concludes] *is, of course, to deprive men of their work and therefore of their earnings. ... In other words, to keep the workers poor or make them poorer is the way to bring on a revolutionary situation.*' Clutterbuck, op. cit., pp.158-9

7   It was in recognition of this dissonance between revolutionary elitism and parliamentary democracy that many Communist parties in Western Europe transformed themselves, with great effect, into 'Euro-Communists' with reforming, left-of-centre programmes.

8   In post-1815 France, radicals like Louis Auguste Blanqui advocated revolution by dedicated, tightly organised cells working on behalf of 'the people'. However their form of direct action was more spontaneous, less systematically planned than that of the Bolsheviks and subsequent 'Marxist-Leninist' movements. Tkachev and his comrades who predated Lenin identified themselves variously as 'nihilists', anarchists and 'social revolutionaries'. The theory of the revolutionary vanguard was at least as characteristic of the Chinese as the Soviet revolutionary experience. It is also, if anything, more pronounced in the Trotskyite parties and 'groupuscles' that have survived and grown since the Soviet Union's downfall. In the revived anarchism of the early twenty-first century, there are also strong 'vanguardist' elements, although the overall strategy is confused to the point of schizophrenia.

9   The two catergories are not, of course, mutually exclusive.

10 By 'far left' here, I am not in general referring to orthodox Communists, or to Marxists of the more thoughtful variety. I refer principally to the radical movements of the 1960s and beyond, based more on appeal to emotion or mob passion than reasoned analysis of the economy and society. It is this New Left and many of the single-issue campaigns that stemmed from it that laid the foundations for today's pseudo-liberalism. I shall also use 'the left' as a generic term, including Marxism, old and new, and varying shades of 'progressive' opinion.

11 Attendant to that is the bizarre assumption that male homosexuals have the same needs and interests as female homosexuals or the equally strange idea that there can be such a thing as 'the Asian community' when British Asians are divided along linguistic, religious and caste lines which can often produce active antagonism.

12 When questioned about his party's increasing commitment to group rights, a parliamentary candidate for the Liberal Democrats told me: 'we have very noisy people putting forward these agendas, and saying that this is what we must do. We can't oppose them because we're afraid to look bad.'

13 In politically correct circles, 'black' (or 'Black') does not necessarily mean of African origin. Increasingly, it is used as a lumping-together word for anyone who is 'non-white'.

14 There are two other tactics are favoured increasingly by single-issue activists, and deployed with particular effect against members of 'their'

identity groups. The first is the benign, cultish smile accompanied by a bland phrase such as 'I'm sorry you feel that way'. The second is to affect personal injury: 'I'm so hurt that you think that'. Both are based on a refusal to take on opponents in debate and so dismiss the possibility of an alternative view. Alternative views, indeed, are reduced to the level of 'feelings', which can be ignored. These ways of 'dealing with' opponents can be more devastating than aggression, although when opponents refuse to be ignored, aggression will follow.

15 Worse still are those men who are dissatisfied with their sexual orientation and seek to change it through voluntary therapy. Regardless of their reasons, or the form of therapy they choose, they are regarded as at once victims to be 'saved' and as enemies to be defeated and reviled. One such man told me that, in the United States especially, 'Therapists who attempt to treat men like me receive death threats from activists'.

16 One of the main criticisms of 'positive discrimination' or 'affirmative action' campaigns on both sides of the Atlantic comes from their alleged beneficiaries. Talented women and black people often feel that their positions, earned on merit, are de-legitimated by such schemes. Significantly, the successful Californian referendum campaign to repeal State affirmative action laws was known as the Civil Rights Initiative and led by African-Americans.

17 The assumption that there is a unified 'white Western culture' is itself as racist as colonial generalisations about African societies or segregationist stereotypes of 'the black man'.

18 That is to say, there has never been a 'Trotskyist regime' as such. Trotskyists often claim to identify with the decentralised forms of socialism, especially when they are politically weak. However the behaviour of Trotsky as Lenin's lieutenant would appear to belie this claim: in the Bolshevik revolution's early years, he ruthlessly crushed a sailors' rebellion (which sought greater freedom) and presided over an immensely repressive system of 'War Communism'. Trotskyite behaviour in trade unions, political parties and campaigns (including single-issue 'identity' movements) is hardly noted for flexibility, tolerance or respect for democracy. We can presume fairly, therefore, that a Trotskyist regime would be a dictatorship.

19 Those experts rarely, if ever, had to live in the flats and estates they designed. There is a story, perhaps apocryphal but probably true, of a Glasgow town planner who declared: 'When you're draining a swamp, you don't consult the frogs'.

20 This means governments at both federal and provincial levels. See *Canada's Tibet: The Killing of the Innu* (London: Survival International, 1999).

21 The German Social Democratic Party (SPD) speaks in similar terms. Its attempt to find a 'New Middle' parallels New Labour's quest for a 'Third Way', between untrammelled capitalism and restrictive state socialism.

22 This leads to the truism that there is no such thing as an 'extreme moderate'.

23 These anxieties are by no means confined to liberals. Democratic socialists have told me that they feel they 'have to support' the demands of feminist and gay groups. Conservatives (both small and large 'c') can be highly defensive about the charge that they are reactionary or out of touch.

Chapter 2

1 This was, of course, the first principle of *Apartheid*, for many years the *bête noire* of politically correct campaigners. Under that system, the state decided who was 'white', 'black' or 'coloured'. Group rights activists follow the same reasoning as *Apartheid*, because they do not respect the individual's freedom to choose his own group.

2 Here 'the state' need not mean the nation-state, or national institutions. International bodies, such as the European Union, the Council of Europe and the United Nations, have become the most zealous champions of group rights. This might be because they are less inhibited than national governments by local custom, cultural precedent or democratic accountability. Increasingly, group rights and internationalism enjoy a symbiotic relationship.

3 Only selected 'minorities' are beneficiaries of 'positive action', or discrimination in reverse. Schemes aimed at 'minority ethnic groups' are rarely held to encompass Jews or Chinese, although they constitute discernible minority populations. Reverse discrimination can also operate in favour of majorities and against minorities, as in the case of post-*Apartheid* South Africa. Religion, denomination and caste have also become criteria for discrimination in reverse, in Northern Ireland and India, for example.

4 This form of pressure group politics extends well beyond interest group politics. In Britain, for example, the Ramblers Association makes extravagant claims to be 'working for walkers', although most of those who enjoy country walking have no interest in trespassing on property or antagonising farmers.

5 As noted above, supporters of outing often use puritanical 'they had it coming' arguments to justify their actions against politicians, clergy and others who might stand in their way. With totalitarian callousness,

however, they fail to consider the families and friends of the individuals they 'expose'. Thus what purports to be an act of individual retribution is in fact an act of collective punishment.

6 In this context, it is interesting to note that Fidel Castro applied the principle of re-education to sexual 'deviants' after he seized power in Havana in 1959. Homosexual men from the capital were sent to work in the fields because Castro believed that 'in the countryside, there is no homosexuality'. Thought reform is still used in nominally Communist China, principally against practitioners of the Falun Gong religion.

7 This incomprehension, of course, extends well beyond the 'gay rights' groups and politically incorrect homosexuals of this case study. Race relations activists respond with similar anger and dismay to 'ungrateful' black people and feminists refuse to accept that some women prefer supposedly 'patriarchal' structures to one-size-fits-all 'equality'.

8 Often that means refusing to accept that 'human nature' really exists. Human behaviour, it is assumed (against all evidence) is socially conditioned and so human beings are infinitely malleable.

9 This is despite the best efforts of the European Commission, whose bureaucracies assiduously promote racial and 'gender' politics.

10 When I pointed this out to Jeff, he merely replied: 'Yes, but it's different. We're talking about equality.'

11 These laws remained on the statute book when the colonies became States, were introduced in new States and in many instances remain on the statute books today.

12 The McCarthyite 'witch hunt' of the early Cold War USA also, as its popular sobriquet suggests, reflects the Puritan spirit. Politically correct campaigners have in recent times revived this spirit of 'exposing' and suppressing dissent, especially at campus level in the United States, where opponents of 'gender' feminism and cultural relativism are muted and where academics announce their 'conversion' to politically correct causes. In British universities, the new Puritan spirit is reflected in frequent student campaigns for 'No Platform' policies to proscribe speakers deemed 'racist' or 'fascist' by the left. Such campaigns have been successful in many campuses, but in others they have been overturned by referendum, proving that a majority of 'real' students believe strongly in freedom of speech.

13 In the late 1990s, Britain's Ministry of Defence also ran a campaign against 'perceived sexism', based also largely on confessions to thought crimes.

14 In the case of the former, the ideal is a language bereft of bawdiness or profanities. In the case of the 'latter', the ideal is an emasculated 'inclu-

sive' language, which places ideological content before elegance or clarity.

15 Jeff interpreted friendships between homosexual and heterosexual men as evidence of 'internalised homophobia' on the part of the former. This is not a novel view, but quite widespread amongst gay activists, who (aping feminists) portray 'straight males' as opponents in a struggle. This equation of personal friendship with treason against group 'identity' gives us quite profound insights into the way politically correct campaigners work, and into the kind of society they wish to create. Their interpretation of friendship should also be seen as comic and bizarre: the phrase 'not sleeping with the enemy' springs to mind.

16 In this broad category, I include individual US states and provinces such as Northern Ireland.

17 Examples of the first include the US federal government, whilst the European Union, in the direction in which it is currently moving, best exemplifies the second.

18 This balkanisation is encouraged and reinforced by identity politics, and the bureaucracies that focus on group rights rather than civil society.

19 Quoted in Betty Yorburg, *Utopia and Reality: A Collective Portrait of American Socialists* (New York & London: Columbia University Press, 1969), p.50

20 Clutterbuck, *op.cit.*, p.177

21 Paul Allender, *What's Wrong With Labour?* (London: Merlin Press, 2001), p.144

22 Christina Hoff Sommers, in her research on boys and young men, cites sociologist David Blankenhorn's conclusion in his book *Fatherless America: Confronting Our Most Urgent Social Problem* (New York: Basic Books, 1995): 'Despite the difficulty of proving causation in social sciences, the wealth of evidence increasingly supports the conclusion that fatherlessness is a primary generator of violence among young men' (p31). Sommers also refers to a study by William Galston (a former domestic adviser to the Clinton administration, now at the University of Maryland) and Elaine Karmack, a lecturer at the J.F. Kennedy School of Government at Harvard. Galston and Karmack write of the relationship between crime in young men and single-mother households that "The relationship is so strong that controlling for family configuration erases the relationship between race and crime and between low income and crime." See Elaine Ciulla Karmack and William Galston, *Putting Children First: A Progressive Family Policy for the 1990s* (Washington, DC: Progressive Policy Institute, 1990), p14.

In 1998, Sommers reports, 'when Cynthia Harper of the University of Pennsylvania and Sara McLanahan of Princeton University studied the incarceration rates of six thousand males aged fourteen to twenty-two between 1979 and 1993. Boys who have lived in homes without fathers were twice as likely to have spent time in jail. These results held even after the researchers controlled for race, income, and parents' education. (Having a stepfather did *not* decrease the likelihood of incarceration). (Harper and McLanahan, 'Father Absence and Youth Incarceration, American Sociological Association, San Francisco, August 1998).

'Fathers,' Sommers concludes, 'appear to be central in helping sons develop a conscience and a sense of responsible manhood. Fathers teach boys that being manly need not mean being predatory or aggressive. By contrast, when the father is absent, male children tend to get the idea of what means to be a man from their peers. Fathers play an indispensable civilizing role in the social ecosystem; therefore, fewer fathers, more male violence.'

[Christina Hoff Sommers, *The War Against Boys; How Misguided Feminism is Harming Our Young Men* (New York: Simon & Schuster, 2000), pp.130-131.]

It must be emphasised here that none of the research cited above is intended to stigmatise single mothers, or underrate the success of many of them against considerable social and economic odds. The reports referred to by Dr Sommers are either politically neutral or from the centre-left of politics.

23 See chapter 6.

24 To both market fundamentalists and politically correct campaigners, motherhood is an impediment: to economic productivity and 'gender' feminism, respectively. The devaluation of motherhood runs parallel to the idea that anyone has a 'right' to a child, although only the most callous would argue that any person has the 'right' to own a dog, for example. The 'right to a child' argument is used to justify commercial surrogacy and demands for lesbian insemination or adoption. In this way, the child – and childbirth itself – is reduced to an instrument of political struggle.

25 Alexis de Tocqueville [Introduction by Hugh Brogan], *The Ancien Regime and the French Revolution* (Manchester: Fontana, 1966, pp179-180.

26 Tocqueville, op. cit., p.180. Tocqueville does not name the Economist in question, but mentions that his plans were carried out forty years later, after the Revolution of 1789.

27 The EU's 'Charter of Fundamental Rights' (2000) expresses well the new liberal agenda of group rights.

Chapter 3

1   A Trotskyist newspaper seller once told me that 'real socialism has never been tried anywhere in the world, except in the Soviet Union during the early 1920s'.

2   The Trotskyist movement in Britain is divided between those who – like the Socialist Workers Party – regard the former Soviet-style regimes as 'state capitalist' and those who – like the Workers Revolutionary Party and its offshoots – view them as 'flawed workers' states'

3   Throughout the text, the terms 'left' and 'right' are used only as a matter of convenience, or because certain individuals and movements identify closely with them. I am aware of the problems caused by these classifications, and refer to such problems wherever it is appropriate or relevant to do so.

4   John Howard Griffin, *Black Like Me* was published in 1961. I cannot remember the exact nature of Mr Griffin's medical treatment, but recall that a course of tablets was involved.

5   Douglas Hyde, a Communist who converted to Catholicism during the war years, recalls in an absorbing book called *I Believed* his pride at media references to 'the four parties'. The Soviet Union's role as an Allied power gave British Communism a 'respectability' it had not previously enjoyed, and which translated temporarily into votes. In 1945, the CP won two Parliamentary seats, but lost them five years later, by which time the Cold War was in full swing.

6   Chairman's Address to the Fourth Annual Conference of Common Wealth, Easter 1946, p.6

7   Another potentially dangerous Common Wealth policy was support for world federalism, which meant that nation-states would be abolished. Significantly, Acland described the nation as 'a sanguinary anachronism dividing those whom a world economy would otherwise unite' (Chairman's Address, 1946, p.7). To be fair, the failure of multi-national states was less apparent in the late 1940s, whilst multi-national corporations had less political and economic clout.

8   The distinction between liberalism and pseudo-liberalism is discussed at greater length in Chapter 5.

9   PNL is now the University of North London.

10 Keith Jacka, Caroline Cox and John Marks, *Rape of Reason: The Corruption of the Polytechnic of North London* (Enfield, Middlesex: Churchill Press Limited, 1975), pp.112-113.

11 Bill Devall, *Simple in Means, Rich in Ends: Practicing Deep Ecology*

(London: Green Print, 1990), p.123. To be fair to Devall, he is summarising the ideas of Patricia Mische, 'an activist and teacher'. To be equally fair to Ms Mische, she is cited as believing that 'there is no good reason for women to push for equal opportunity to serve in Titan missile silos or as bomber pilots or to build advanced nuclear weapons (in Devall, op. cit., p.123). This distances her from the 'unisexist' feminism promoted by most politically correct campaigners, although it is likely that she disapproves of male military culture of all kinds on ideological grounds. Elsewhere in the book, Devall shows awareness of the divisive impact of feminism on the ecology movement when he argues that: *We need to move beyond conflicts between genders to search for experience which will encourage an ethic of caring for the earth* (Devall, op. cit., p. 57). However he does not develop from this a coherent critique of 'ecofeminism'. Perhaps, like too many green campaigners, he is more nervous of social than economic orthodoxies.

12 David Fernbach, 'Ten Years of Gay Liberation', in Diana Adlam, Beatrix Campbell et. al., *Politics and Power, Volume Two* (London, Boston and Henley: Routledge & Kegan Paul, 1980), p.178. Fernbach is summarising the 'key theoretical elements' in the London Gay Liberation Front *Manifesto* of 1971. The Manifesto 'was drafted by a group of lesbians and gay men who came mainly from a Marxist background' (Fernbach, op.cit.) and were influenced by the American New Left. The ideas contained in it still inform the gay movement, in both its 'mainstream' and 'radical' aspects.

13 London Gay Liberation Front *Manifesto*, quoted in Fernbach, op. cit., p.177

14 David Frawley, an expert on Vedic Indian thought, has pointed out to me that in India, when governments introduced caste-based 'affirmative action', many well-established castes of craftsmen redefined themselves as 'lower' castes to qualify for aid. In his many books, he emphasises that the ancient caste system was more fluid than that of more recent Hinduism – and less rigid than the politically correct categories of authoritarian liberalism.

15 Christina Hoff Sommers, *Who Stole Feminism? How Women Have Betrayed Women* (New York: Simon & Schuster, 1994), p. 260

16 Jack, Cox and Marks, op. cit., p.48

17 ibid., p.49

18 ibid, p.49

19 Anthony Arblaster, *Academic Freedom* (Harmondsworth; Penguin, 1974), pp.165-6.

20 See Chapter 4, 'The New Stereotypes' for a fuller discussion of 'false consciousness' theory and its influence on politically correct campaigners.

21 In the case of the old left, it was a united front against capitalism or fascism.

22 The same paradox existed in the Labour movement, where the social conservatism of working-class communities conflicted with the bohemian values of middle-class activists. This conflict intensified in the closing decades of the twentieth century, when bohemianism gave way to politically correct hostility to the 'traditional family'.

23 For the best account of the development of black cultures in Britain, and the tensions between those cultures and 'anti-racist' activism, see Roy Kerridge, *The Story of Black History* (London: Claridge Press, 1998). Kerridge describes the way in which 'progressive' teachers drew no distinctions between the experience of Afro-Caribbeans in Britain and African-Americans, despite marked cultural and historical differences. He also refers to black parents who send their children to live with relations in the Caribbean, so that they can receive a 'traditional British schooling' no longer available in the United Kingdom.

24 Fernbach, op. cit., p.174. The only ideological perspectives cited are variations on a Marxist theme.

25 Similar charges are made by 'anti-racists' against non-militant black people, by feminists against anti-feminist women and by Marxists against conservative working-class men and women.

26 By 'idealised', I mean idealised in feminist terms. That is to say, the idealised feminist conception is of women who wish to live independently of men, or wish to dissolve existing differences between the sexes.

27 Chancellor Williams, *The Destruction of Black Civilization* (Chicago: Third World Press, 1987), p.315. Cited in George B.N. Ayittey, *Indigenous African Institutions* (Ardley-on-Hudson, New York: Transnational Publishers, Inc., 1991) p. xxxv

Chapter 4

1 Similarly, a far right movement in the United States that combines racism, anti-Semitism and Protestant fundamentalism calls itself 'Christian Identity'. The expression of the abortion debate in simplistic terms of right, simplifies an important moral and political question, making compromise on either side less possible.

2 Fernbach, op.cit., p.185

3 The actions of such men should of course be regarded as rights exercised

by members of a free society. However they have been met with violent protests, intimidation and threats from the activist movement.

4 Francesca Klug, *Values for a Godless Age: The Story of the United Kingdom's New Bill of Rights* (Harmondsworth: Penguin, 2000). Dr Klug's book is far more measured and thoughtful than its title implies. She acknowledges the role of religious and spiritual, as well as secular values in framing such charters as the Universal Declaration of Human Rights and the European Convention for the Protection of Human Rights and Fundamental Freedoms in the years following World War II.

5 In particular, 'first-past-the-post' voting creates disproportionate House of Commons majorities and encourages two-party polarisation instead of the consensus that most voters favour.

6 These circumstances include illegal abortion, with its cruel profiteering and dangerous medical implications, or compelling women to give birth as a result of rape.

7 The most famous example of this scapegoating is perhaps Clarence Thomas, the African American Supreme Court Justice who opposes 'affirmative action' (reverse discrimination) and so is vilified by white and black 'liberals' alike.

8 Jacka, Cox, Marks, op. cit., p.40

9 This quotation from Justice Jackson was cited to me in private correspondence with Dr Stephen Baskerville, Anglo-American political scientist and lobbyist on behalf of divorced fathers in the United States.

10 Richard Clutterbuck, *Protest and the Urban Guerrilla* (London: Cassell, 1973), p.260

11 Edward Goldsmith, *Blueprint for Survival* (Harmondsworth: Pelican, 1971), p.64

12 Clutterbuck, op.cit., pp.176-7

Chapter 5

1 T.W. Adorno, Else Frenkel-Brunswikk, Daniel J. Levinson and R. Nevitt Sanford, *The Authoritarian Personality* (John Wiley and Sons: New York, 1964 edition), pp.181-2; passim. For a critique of *The Authoritarian Personality*, see Christopher Lasch, *The True and Only Heaven* (?), pp. ? Lasch's criticisms of Adorno et al are relevant to this discussion, in that he accuses them, in effect, of authoritarian liberalism. This is because they take their analysis beyond the political to the personal, and in particular the psychological. The 'authoritarian [right-wing] personality' is therefore treated as a psychiatric patient, whose political opinions are

'symptoms' of mental disease. Both implicitly and explicitly, there is a psychologically correct form of politics, that of the 'liberal-left'. I share these criticisms of Adorno's theory and methodology. However *The Authoritarian Personality* contains some valuable political insights, from which we might legitimately draw in examining *pseudo-liberalism.*

2   For a critique of 'Neolithic' feminism, see Janet Biehl, *Rethinking Ecofeminist Politics* (Boston; South End Press, 19')), pp.29-57

3   The phrase 'ever-closer union' was used in the Treaty of Rome (1958), which brought the European 'common market' into being. This was intended to mean an ever-closer union of nation-states whose political and economic interests would (it was assumed) overlap. The phrase was repeated in the Treaty of Nice (2000), whose preamble speaks of an 'ever-closer union of Europe's peoples'. The inclusion of 'Europe's peoples' is at one level pragmatic, for it creates the impression of democratic consent. At another level, it represents an effort, ideologically-based, to shift the emphasis of European politics away from the nation-state.

4   Vine Deloria, Jr, 'On Liberation', in *For This Land: Writings On Religion In America* (London: Routledge, 1999), p.102

5   A similar situation pertained to religion in Northern Ireland, where questions about denomination discriminated against the Roman Catholic minority. Now such questions are back, to serve a dual but contradictory purpose: eliminating 'religious discrimination' and imposing sectarian quotas.

6   See Todd Gitlin, *The Twilight of Common Dreams: Why America Is Wracked by Culture Wars* (New York: Metropolitan Books [Henrey Holt and Company], 1995).

7   The European Commission actively supports reverse sex discrimination in employment. This right to discriminate is enshrined in the European Union's 'Charter of Rights' in (needless to say) the section concerned with non-discrimination and 'equality'.

8   *Sesame* (Open University magazine), December 1972, p.16. Quoted in Keith Jacka, Caroline Cox, John Marks, *Rape of Reason: The Corruption of the Polytechnic of North London* (Enfield: Churchill Press Limited, 1975), p.43. Dr Rose's views have probably changed since then, but such politically correct attacks or scientific 'hierarchy' have become commonplace.

9   Quoted in Gitlin, *Twilight of Common Dreams*, op. cit., p.226

10 Michael J. Priore, *Beyond Individualism* (Cambridge, Mass: Harvard University Press, 1995), p.146

11 Gitlin, op.cit., p.226

12 The British Armed Forces now have an 'Armed Forces Lesbian and Gay Association', which seeks to impose a group rights agenda on service-men, and issues rigid, cult-like propaganda about 'equality'.

13 Mary Miles, The Observer (London), 1 August 1971. Quoted in Richard Clutterbuck, *Protest and the Urban Guerrilla* (London: Cassell, 1973), p.1 76

14 Soren Hansen and Jesper Jensen, *The Little Red Schoolbook* [British edition, tr. Bent Thomberry] (London: Stage 1, 1971). The book was convicted under the Obscene Publications Act in 1971. This is reflected in my edition, where a few sections have been rewritten.

15 *The Little Red Schoolbook*, op. cit., p.89

16 ibid.

17 ibid

18 ibid.

19 Dancing classes are attacked because 'they try to get you to behave in such a way that grown-ups will think you're "nice young people".'

20 ibid, p.95: *'People who warn you against both strong feelings and sex are as a rule afraid of both Although boys and girls become sexually mature much earlier these days, the "age of consent" for girls is still 16. Our laws assume that boys under 14 simply aren't capable of fucking.'*

21 An acquaintance of this author was threatened with disciplinary action when he held the door for a female colleague. He was employed by one of London's most left-wing borough councils at the time.

22 Brian Mitchell, *Women in the Military. Flirting With Disaster* (Washington, DC: Regnery Publishing, Inc., 1998), pp. 342-3

23 ManKind web site: http://www.mankind.org.uk

Chapter 6

1 In previous chapters, I have used Christina Hoff Sommers' valuable dis-tinction between 'equity' feminism and 'gender' feminism. In this chapter, I use the umbrella term 'feminism', for three reasons. First, I wish to avoid excessively cumbersome definitions and sub-groupings. Secondly, there are more than a few instances where the distinction has become blurred or is hard to discern. Thirdly, the chapter looks at the way in which feminist ideology contributes to what I have called 'unisexism'. Both the 'equity' and the 'gender' components can sometimes point us in that dirtection.

2 Female critics of feminism come from a variety of political backgrounds. In Britain, they include Erin Pizzey and Melanie Phillips, who began

their careers on the left of politics and still identify with a 'progressive' tradition. In the United States, the most prominent anti-feminist woman is probably Phyllis Schlafly, a staunchly conservative commentator who helped prevent the 'Equal Rights Amendment' in the early 1980s, because it placed equality before freedom. Ironically, the political career of Phyllis Schlafly resembles closely the lifestyle of the 'career women' she roundly berates. More recently, Christina Hoff Sommers has opposed feminist dogma from a very liberal democratic perspective.

3   'Western Civilisation' was a course taken by most American undergraduate students until recent times. It is being replaced, increasingly, by 'cultural studies' courses that are largely an attack on culture, Western or otherwise.

4   It is worth noting that 'Western culture' is described by these ideologues as if it were a monolithic structure, rather than a series of intersecting circles. Ironically, they thus echo false Western generalisations about 'Africa', 'the East' or 'Islam'.

5   In Britain, the move towards 'comprehensive' education and the expansion of universities reflects a similar pattern of thought, and has had similar social consequences.

6   David Riesman, Nathan Glazer and Reuel Denney, *The Lonely Crowd: A Study of the Changing American Character* (Garden City, NY: Doubleday Anchor Books, 1953 edition), p.93

7   An assumption parallel to that of group rights, and possibly related to it, is the idea that a corporation has the status of 'a person' in law, and so is accorded the rights and protections traditionally accorded to individuals. This concept of corporation-as-person is most fully developed under American law, and it is in the United States that the idea of group rights has been most politically pervasive.

8   These denunciations operate on an 'equal opportunity' basis, against opponents of whichever ethnic background, sex or sexual orientation.

9   The 'all-women shortlists' adopted by the British Labour Party before the 1997 election are a classic example, as is the idea that fifty per cent of State delegates to party Conventions should automatically be women.

10   Michael Levin, 'Comparable Worth: The Feminist Road to Socialism', *Commentary*, Vol. 74, no. 3 (September 1984), pp. 13-19; 'Comparable Worth' chapter in *Feminism and Freedom* (New Brunswick, NJ: Transaction Books, 1987), pp.137-142

11   Erin Pizzey founded the first shelter for battered women in Britain. Her sin, in feminist eyes, was to examine the complexities surrounding domestic violence, and so help real women and real men, rather than accept an ideological line that defied her experience.

12 It is worth noting here that Marx never considered himself a 'Marxist', and indeed objected to that label.

13 Engels, quoted in Janet Coleman, *Against the State: Studies in Sedition and Rebellion* (London: BBC Books, 1990), p.187

14 Quoted in Christina Hoff Sommers, *Who Stole Feminism? How Women Have Betrayed Women* (New York: Touchstone Books, 1995), pp.256-7

15 Robert Bly, *The Sibling Society* (London: Hamish Hamilton, 1996), p.175

16 Bly, op. cit., p. 175

17 The pervasive nature of unisexist propaganda is evidenced by the following letter in The Daily Telegraph, an almost notoriously conservative newspaper, published 27 October 2000. It concerns attempts to force the Carlton Club, associated with the Tory Party, to accept women as full members, even though eighty per cent of 'lady associate members' wished to retain the *status quo:*

Sir – The problem with women such as Yvonne Clifford, who are perfectly "content with the way things are" at the Carlton Club, enjoying the right to pay half the subscription of male associate membership (letter, Oct. 23), is that they do a tremendous damage to women who wish to be treated as equals.

It is all too easy to be regarded as acceptable in an inferior role. Women in golf clubs have done this for almost a century, paying a lower subscription and then being faced with restricted tee times, no voting rights and a men's bar.

"Ladies" collude. Women have a better sense of their own identity and assert themselves. Liz Kahn, Barnet, Herts

Note the assumption that these ladies have a duty to their sex, defined by feminists. Their expressed wishes, because they conflict with feminist goals, can be dictatorially overruled. Note too that Miss Kahn uses 'lady' as a term of abuse (like 'scab' or 'class traitor') and that she makes the totalitarian assumption that private clubs are public property.

18 'Women get the call-up,' *Daily Telegraph*, London, 25 October 2000. In the UK, unlike the USA, the frontline Infantry and Special Forces have retained the right only to recruit men.

19 For a full history of feminist pressure on the US Armed Forces, and its negative effects on the discipline and morale of men, see Brian Mitchell, *Women in the Military: Flirting With Disaster* (Washington, DC: Regnery Publishing, Inc., 1998).

20 Judith M. Bardwick, *In Transition: How Feminism, Sexual Liberation and the Search for Self-Fulfillment have Altered Our Lives* (New York: Holt, Rinehart and Winston, 1979), p.15

21 Lord Hunt of Llanfair Waterdine (ed), *In Search of Adventure: A Study of Opportunities for Adventure and Challenge for Young People* (Guildford, Surrey; Talbot Adair Press, undated but early 1980s).

22 It was pressure from feminists that led the Mothers Union to accept men as members. The Hunt Report, cited above, speaks of girls' strong interest in equestrian pursuits as if that was something to be lamented, rather than something good.

Chapter 7

1 Filippo Tomasso Marinetti, Futurism's principal spokesman, was also a founder member of the Italian Fascisti.

2 This federation of unions later abandoned anarcho-syndicalism and backed the French Communist Party.

3 Georges Sorel, *Refelxions sur la violence* (Paris, 1908), quoted in Larry Portis, *Sorel* (London: Pluto Press Limited, 1980), p.58

4 Irving Louis Horowitz, 'American Radicalism and the Revolt Against Reason', in Horowitz, *Ideology and Utopia in the United States, 1956-1976* (Oxford: Oxford University Press, 1977), pp. 180-194. Horowitz notes a renewed interest in Sorel and anarcho-syndicalism, during the 1960s student protest. He notes too some similarities between syndicalists and the New Left, such as rejection of orthodox Marxism, stress on emotion above reason and intense hostility to the liberal state. The 1960s New Left was the precursor to more recent ideologies of group rights, including feminism.

5 For a discussion of the relationship between the fascist Corporate State and 'politically correct' ideas of representation by race, 'gender', sexual orientation, etc., see Chapter One.

6 Noel O'Sullivan, Fascism (London: J.M. Dent & Sons Ltd, 1983), p. 138. O'Sullivan is quoting from Hitler's conversation in 1934 with Herman Rauschnig, a traditionalist conservative.

7 Hitler, quoted in O'Sullivan, op. cit., p. 139

8 Hazel Henderson, *Paradigms in Progress: Life Beyond Economics* (London: Adamantine Press Limited, 1993), p.140

9 George L. Mosse, *The Crisis of German Ideology: Intellectual Origins of the Third Reich* (New York: Schocken Books, 1981 edition), p.15

10 Mary Field Belenky, Blythe McVicker Clinchy, Nancy Rule Goldberger and Jill Mattuck Tarule, *Women's Ways of Knowing* (New York: Basic Books, 1986), p. 104. Quoted in Christina Hoff Sommers, *Who Stole Feminism? How Women Have Betrayed Women* (New York: Touchstone, 1995), p.67

11 Peggy, McIntosh, 'Seeing Our Way Clear: Feminist Revision and the Academy'. Quoted in Hoff Sommers, op. cit., p.67. The choice of the phrase 'feminist revision' is also interesting, given the popularity of 'historical revision' amongst neo-Nazi groups, and their euphemistic, pseudo-scholastic use of that term.

12 There is another type of ecofeminism, promoted by such thinkers as the Indian activist Vandana Shiva and the Swedish 'counter-development' expert Helena Norberg-Hodge. We can refer to this, in Hoff Sommers' terms, as 'equity' ecofeminism, for it is about restoring a natural balance between the sexes, not waging a sex struggle against the male. Equity ecofeminists like Shiva are also concerned to preserve the best aspects of traditional cultures, including those that honour women and motherhood and not create a unisex society. The ecofeminism considered below is therefore 'gender' ecofeminism, a Western-based new liberal dogma that uses green issues to camouflage and anti-male political agenda.

13 Valerie Plumwood, quoted in Andrew Dobson, *Green Political Thought* (London; Routledge, 1995), p.194

14 This last choice phrase is quoted in Bly, op. cit., p.175

15 The inclusion of old German beliefs in an anti-Semitic ideology makes little sense, when we remember that there was no Jewish presence in central Europe when the Germans worshipped Wotan and Thunor.

16 Hazel Henderson, 'Beyond the New Paradigm', in John Button (ed), *The Green Fuse: The Schumacher Lectures*, 1983-8I (London: Quartet Books, 1990), p.123

17 ibid., p.123

18 ibid., p.123

19 Mosse, op.cit., p.72

20 ibid., pp.71-2. Mosse records that von Leers spent his post-War exile in Egypt, where (not surprisingly, perhaps) he refined his philosophy as sun worship and its connection with National Socialism.

21 Henderson, in Button, op.cit., pp.124-5

22 Expressions of individual consciousness, Henderson argues, are expressions of patriarchal 'duality'. National Socialism postulated a similar theory of individual consciousness as worthless in comparison to 'folk-consciousness'.

23 Mussolini also believed that the question of balance between individual freedom and state power was 'old-fashioned', like representative democracy or equality before the law. Indeed the state could be seen as the expression of a national genotype:

The State is not only present, it is also past, and above all future. It is the state which, transcending the brief limit of individual lives, represents the immanent conscience of the nation. Quoted in Anthony Arblaster and Stephen Lukes (eds), *The Good Society: A Book of Readings* (London: Methuen & Co ltd, 1971), pp.314-15. Once again, the parallels with Henderson's phenotype-genotype theory are quite remarkable.

24 This conception of the free individual is not, of course, confined to Western culture. In Hinduism and Buddhism, for example, the idea of *karma* implies an individual's responsibility for his actions, and the effect that some actions might have on future incarnations. Confucianism emphasises individual responsibility, as in a very different way does Islam, and as do Native American hero myths and the Germanic sagas which the Nazis defiled. These areas, although interesting to pursue, lie largely outside the scope of this study.

25 Here the feminist arguments in support of abortion on demand are interesting. At one level, there is the assertion of 'rights', expressed through the rhetoric of 'a woman's right to choose'. This appears conventionally socialist, at least in terms of post-1960s 'issue-based' socialism. Yet abortion is defended not as a tragic necessity in certain cases, but as a 'right' by which absolute power over the unborn child may be exercised. To justify that power, the unborn child is described as 'not quite human' or 'not a human being' and therefore having no 'right' to exist. Over the issue of abortion on demand, there emerges another ideological convergence between feminists and National Socialists. Both have a conception of the 'subhuman', which they use to justify the technologically assisted taking of life.

26 In the same way, the multiculturalist identification of reason with 'white' culture revives racist assumptions which have been long discredited.

27 The American feminist Gloria Steinem, for example, believes that boys ought to be 'raised like girls'.

28 Hazel Henderson, *Paradigms in Progress: Life Beyond Economics* (London: Adamantine Press Limited, 1993), p.140

29 Mitchell, op.cit., p.44. The report he summarises, The Integration of Women into a Male Initiation Rite: A Case Study of the USAF Academy', was influenced by the work of Arnold van Gennep, who researched rites of passage in both 'primitive' and 'modern' societies.

Chapter 8

1 At the time of writing, the future of the 'anti-globalisation' movement, always a patchwork coalition of differing interests, is unclear. The 'war on

terrorism' declared by the Western powers is global in scope, draws upon deep-rooted cultural anxieties and might provide a useful pretext for the silencing of critics of the prevailing economic order. On the other hand, the events of September 11th, 2001, and the confused response to them beneath the rhetoric of unity, both demonstrate the vulnerability of the globalist economic model.

2 I am aware that this analogy (used throughout the book) does not do justice to the many humane men and women who served, and sometimes still serve, as Christian missionaries. However the secular missionaries of political correctness usually emulate the least culturally sensitive and most fundamentalist-inclined missionaries of the colonial era. Much as the most dogmatic and ruthless missionaries of those times talked loudly about humility, their 'liberal' descendants preach a gospel of 'human rights'. The underlying premise – 'West knows best' – has remained constant. Unlike missionaries, however, politically correct campaigners do not generally regard themselves as subject to any higher power.

3 See Edward Goldsmith, *Blueprint for Survival* (Harmondsworth: Penguin, 1971) and Edward Goldsmith & Jerry Mander (eds.), The Case Against the Global Economy (London: Earthscan: 2001).

4 The great exception to this are the anarcho-syndicalists, who believe in control of the economy and society by large industrial collectives. See Chapter Seven.

5 Richard Clutterbuck, *Protest and the Urban Guerrilla* (London: Cassell, 1973), p.162

6 In English cities, for example, the most violent 'anti-racist' campaigners tend to be either Trotskyist or anarchist, although the ideological wall between them is paper-thin. Their beliefs are indistinguishable from those of race relations bureaucrats, except that they are prepared to use direct violence against their opponents. In such confrontations, the 'anti-racists' tend to be students and young professionals, whereas the 'racists' tend to be working-class youth of low educational attainment, living in socially deprived areas – once a natural constituency for the left.

7 The US Green Party, for instance, which nominated Ralph Nader as presidential candidate in 2000, opposed laws exempting small and medium-sized companies from 'affirmative action' laws.

8 In the May Day anti-globalisation protests of 2001, a London anarchist group distributed a mock 'monopoly board' of potential 'targets' – although in practice none of them were attacked. They included the Pall Mall clubs, less because they were bastions of 'privilege' and more

because some of them are all-male (see Chapter One). Free association is clearly no longer an anarchist principle, although in a society without law it would surely be hard to prevent.

9 Writing about the British far left in the early 1970s, Richard Clutterbuck says of the Trotskyist International Marxist Group: *The International Marxist Group (IMG) is firmly at the amateur end of the revolutionary spectrum, being almost wholly intellectual and much torn by internal dissensions. … IMG concentrates on arousing minority groups, such as students and coloured immigrants (it has close links with the British Black Power movement) and sees revolution less in terms of workers' control than of a rising of oppressed races in (or having migrated from) the under-developed world. Its work is mainly centred in the universities, which it aims to convert into 'red bases', initially by forming 'red circles' of revolutionary activists. These operate by selecting suitable issues on which they can stir up idealistic students to protest – for example, Vietnam, Biafra or South Africa.* Clutterbuck, op. cit., pp.169-70. IMG's principal activists included the militant feminist Sheila Rowbottom and Tariq Ali, who is now one of the most skilful and articulate left-wing commentators in British politics.

10 This is to promote 'equal opportunity' to compete.

11 Of course there are exceptions to this, both at individual and organisational level (not to admit of exceptions is to fall into the same trap as the politically correct). One such exception is Black Environment Network, which does much to give inner city children (white as well as black) access to the countryside.

12 Richard Body, *England for the English* (London: New European Publications, 2001), pp.177-8.

13 The book deals specifically with England, as distinct from the other constituent nations of the United Kingdom. Body's thesis is that the Scottish and Welsh are asserting their national identities more confidently than England, whose status is ever more ambiguous.

14 This intolerance emerges, as outlined above, when members of minority ethnic groups express opposition to abortion on demand, or raise religious and cultural objections to the gay movement.

15 Benjamin R. Barber, *Jihad vs. McWorld: How Globalism and Tribalism Are Shaping the World* (New York: Ballantine Books, 1996), p.20. Quoted in Oliver Bennett, *Cultural Pessimism: Narratives of Decline in the Postmodern World* (Edinburgh: Edinburgh University Press, 2001), pp.171-2

16 The word 'Taliban' means 'student', reflecting the fundamentalist organisation's origins as a radical student militia.

17 This is true of other types of religious fundamentalism, including some forms of evangelical Christianity.

18 There is an interesting, if somewhat unexpected parallel between the attitudes towards women displayed by radical Islamists and radical – especially lesbian – feminists. The former compel women to appear veiled or covered in public, whereas the latter discourage the use of cosmetics and oppose as 'sexist' traditional – or modern – displays of femininity. For example, the American feminist pioneer (and Communist Party member) Mary Inman wrote in her 1940 book *In Women's Defense* [sic] that traditional child-rearing methods 'manufacture femininity' and that the 'over-emphasis on beauty' is a way of subjugating women. Both approaches, radical Islamist and radical feminist, have in common an austere and extreme sexual Puritanism that constrains the behaviour of heterosexual women.

19 Such societies aim to recruit students unsure of their sexuality in much the same way as evangelical groups 'reach out' to those who are most unsure of their faith.

20 Far left groups, in particular those of Trotskyist origin, have often been compared to small religious sects, in their persistent doctrinal disputes and their cult-like thought control of their membership. Their interpretations of Marxism are nothing if not fundamentalist, but have strongly influenced the liberal-left.

21 George Orwell, 'The Lion and the Unicorn: Socialism and the English Genius' (1940), in *The Penguin Essays of George Orwell* (Harmondsworth: Penguin, 1984), pp.146-7.

Index

Tkachev, Peter, 5
Tocqueville, Alexis de, 33, 34, 36, 94
Trade unions, 39, 83, 85
Trotskyism, 38, 73, 89, 112, 124
'Two Ronnies' (Corbett and
    Barker), 63

Unisex society, as feminist goal, 92-
    108
United Airlines, 84
Utilities, public, 12

Vietnam War, 81

Volkisch movements, pre-Nazi
    Germany, 109-120, 129

Waugh, Evelyn, 123, 129
Webb, Beatrice, 8
Williams, Chancellor, 54
Women's Societies (Native
    American), 2
World Trade Centre, destruction of,
    xiv

Yin and Yang, 68
Yorburg, Betty, 28

Other Books from **New European**

Available to readers at 20% discount.
Send cheques to: New European Publications Limited
14-16 Carroun Road, London SW8 1JT
Tel/Fax ++44 (0) 20 7582 3996

QUESTIONS OF IDENTITY
Exploring the Character of Europe
Edited by Christopher Joyce
ISBN 1-86064-696-4
256 pages   paperback   £14.95
Published in association with IB Tauris.
(Available post free from New European Publications direct.)

What does 'European' mean? European identity has long been hotly debated and a cause of deep division both in political parties and in Britain at large. This book brings together powerful and cutting edge contributions from all sides of the debate over the past three decades from academics, journalists, business people and politicians. Contributors include Ronald Butt, Lord Dahrendorf, Richard Hoggart, Flora Lewis, Cees Nooteboom, Norman Stone and Margaret Thatcher.

A selection of articles from the journal New European. Some radical alternatives for Europe's future.

THE BREAKDOWN OF EUROPE
Richard Body
ISBN 1-8724-1011-1
101 pages   hardback   £9.95

How the European Union will break down in the electronic age and how the other mega states in the world will also disintegrate.

"Sir Richard Body is the most original thinker in today's Conservative Party."
                              Aidan Rankin, *Times Literary Supplement*

THE BREAKDOWN OF NATIONS
Leopold Kohr
ISBN 1-870098-98-6
256 pages   paperback   £9.95
(with a foreword by Richard Body and Neil Ascherson)
Published in association with Green Books.
(Available post free from New European Publications direct.)

Leopold Kohr's seminal work which inspired Schumacher and the whole

Small is Beautiful movement. It argues that people have happier and better lives in smaller states.

"This is the most important work written by the most original thinker of the late 20th century."

Neil Ascherson

EUROPE OF MANY CIRCLES
Constructing a Wider Europe
Richard Body
ISBN 1-8724-1001-4
182 pages   hardback   £14.95

Europe of Many Circles sets out how the European Community can be reshaped into something big enough to serve the people of all Europe, while also small enough in power to allow her people to enjoy both democracy and individual liberty.

"Richard Body's *Europe of Many Circles* is brilliant."

The Telegraph

THE CONSCIENCE OF EUROPE
Edited by John Coleman
ISBN 92-871-4030-8
212 pages   £12.00
Published by the Council of Europe in association with New European Publications

The Council of Europe, which President de Gaulle described as 'that Sleeping Beauty on the banks of the Rhine', is the institution through which the spiritual and moral leadership of Europe should be expressed. Contributors include: Cosmo Russell, Vaclav Havel, Peter Smithers and George Carey.

"The approach to the subject is decidedly spiritual, as befits an examination of conscience, and provides a welcome change from the usual economic or political analyses of the EU..."

Alain Woodrow, *The Tablet*

"Churchmen and statesmen, poets and philosophers, each were asked to contribute a response which might be collated, with the original essay, into a compiled work. The result is truly remarkable - and in truth impossible to review."

James Bourlet, *Britain and Overseas (Economic Research Council)*

"*The conscience of Europe* is a book for both eurosceptics and europhiles. As such I recommend it highly as a means of stimulating the woefully inadequate discussion in Britain about the future of Europe."

Graham Dines, *East Anglia Daily Times*

DISINTEGRATING EUROPE
The Twilight of the European Construction
Noriko Hama
Adamantine Studies on the Changing European Order, No.7
ISBN 0-7449-0122-7
144 pages   hardback   £27.50
ISBN 0-7449-0123-5
144 pages   paperback   £14.50
Published in association with New European Publications.
(Available post free from New European Publications direct.)

"The book has challenged and intensified Japanese interest in Europe's immediate future and opens the way for fresh constructive discussion in Europe itself on how to invigorate the Continent."   George Bull, Editor, *International Minds*

"Presents a clear and exhaustive picture of Europe at a turning-point in its history – the collapse of the post-war system."   *Nichi-ei Times*

THE THROW THAT FAILED
Britain's 1961 Application to Join the Common Market
Lionel Bell
ISBN 1-8724-1003-0
224 pages   paperback   £15.00

Lionel Bell analyses the until recently secret government papers which are now available under the 30-year rule. With a lifetime of experience in the Public Record Office and elsewhere in the Civil Service, including responsibility for the papers of Winston Churchill, he is in a unique position to assemble and weigh all the evidence relating to this issue, which continues to have such momentous consequences for Europe's future.

ENGLAND FOR THE ENGLISH
Richard Body
ISBN 1-8724-1014-6
181 pages   hardback   £13.95

A provocative and controversial but optimistic book about England's future, now that the United Kingdom is breaking up. The English will prosper and their culture – their core values and beliefs – in the electronic age will make them influential in the world. England will always be multiracial, but her unity and future depends upon rejecting multiculturalism.

"Body's solution seems to be a decentralised Europe less like the US and more like Switzerland.   Aidan Rankin, *Times Literary Supplement*

"Sir Richard Body is a politician of unusual intelligence."   *The Daily Telegraph*

CHARLEMAGNE
Douglas Pickett / drawings by Harry Tucker
ISBN 1-8724-1002-2
paperback £2.50

The story of Charlemagne, one of the great Europeans in History, is written for 12-16 year olds but is suitable for all ages.

THE SIMULTANEOUS POLICY
An Insider's Guide to Saving Humanity and the Planet
John Bunzl (with a foreword by Diana Schumacher)
ISBN 1-8724-1015-4
210 pages hardback £14.95

The greatest barrier to solving our global environmental, economic and social problems is destructive competition between nations to attract capital and jobs, harming society and the environment around the world. *The Simultaneous Policy* offers a solution and also outlines a political campaign that transcends party politics and offers the prospect of global transformation and survival.

"It's ambitious and provocative. Can it work? Certainly worth a serious try."
Noam Chomsky

"It's a good idea. What we need is politicians who will give this issue a high priority."
Polly Toynbee, *The Guardian*

"Your proposal … reflects the core ideas of how to create consensus around change. This is the biggest challenge that we have."
Ed Mayo, Executive Director, *New Economic Foundation*

SEVEN STEPS TO JUSTICE
Rodney Shakespeare and Peter Challen
ISBN 1-8724-1027-8
212 pages paperback £10.95

Seven Steps to Justice is an overall rethinking of economics and politics to create a new paradigm providing two basic incomes for all, a proper deal for both halves of humanity and hope for the world.

TONY BLAIR
Making Labour Liberal
David Wells
ISBN 0-907044-05-1
176 pages   paperback   £5.99
Published in association with Rain Press.
(Available post free from New European Publications direct.)

"An exhilaratingly clear analysis of New Labour's half-baked ideology, and the post-modern authoritarianism of the Blair "Project"..."
Aidan Rankin, Deputy Editor, *The New European*

"I am normally wary of reading political books because so often they are badly written and full of weak arguments and academic jargon, but your book has none of these failings and I greatly enjoyed its original analysis of Blair as a Liberal."
Leo McKinstry, author and *Daily Mail* feature writer

"The book's critique of what passes for Blair's philosophy is timely and often acute, especially in its relationship with the neo-liberal agenda of economic globalisation."   Brian Fewster, *Green World*, Winter 2000/1, p 20

YUGOSLAVIA – AN AVOIDABLE WAR
Nora Beloff
ISBN 1-8724-1008-1
150 pages plus 16 photographs   paperback   £12.95

In this outstanding appraisal of the modern history of Yugoslavia and the factors surrounding its break-up, Nora Beloff takes sacred tenets of received wisdom and subjects them to close analysis. Interventions by foreign governments, the role of the United Nations, the recognition of the secessionists' political platforms, together with the diplomatic infighting and confusion are all chronicled in this concise account.

NURTURING THE NATURAL LAWS OF PEACE
Through Regional Peace and Development Programmes
ISBN 1-872410-25-1
132 pages   paperback   £10.95

The book is founded on the idea of international law based on co-operation, social, economic and political human rights, as enshrined in the UN Charter. Something like regional Marshall Plans are needed fro the poorer areas of the world, especially today if there is to be any hope of stemming the tide of terrorism.

THE WITHERED GARLAND
Reflections and Doubts of a Bomber
Peter Johnson
ISBN 1-8724-1004-9
370 pages plus photographs   hardback   £20.00

The story of a RAF pilot who commanded Lancaster squadrons in the Second World War who began to doubt the idea that the best way to win wars was to terrorise civilian populations.

"One of the most important books of the twentieth century."   Bruce Kent

RETRIEVED FROM THE FUTURE
John Seymour
ISBN 1-8724-1005-7
235 pages   paperback   £10.00

John Seymour imagines a crash of the structure of Government in Britain and gives a chilling but realistic description of how a federation of East Anglia survives. The recent emergency procedures following the collapse of the South East Asian economies suggest that Seymour is fairly near the mark in his vivid description of life in such circumstances.

COLEMAN'S DRIVE
John Coleman
ISBN 1-8724-1006-5
260 pages plus illustrations   paperback   £10.00

This is the true story of a ride from Buenos Aires to New York in a 1925 Austin 7 'Chummy' through the mountains, deserts and jungles of South and Central America.

"Coleman's Drive with its implied challenge to a classic of travel is, like its author, tough cool and daring."

"His fantastic journey had to be improvised in short stretches of guesswork on the edge of risk."   *Times Literary Supplement*

"Coleman's book is a fascinating account of a fascinating journey."   *The Guardian*

"This is one of the best travel books of recent times."   *Motor Sport*

CHASING GHOSTS
Brian Milton
ISBN 1-8724102-3-5
224 pages   hardback   £16.99

The story of an attempt to cross the Atlantic by Microlight, by the author of the famous *Global Flyer*.

SOD'EM AT GOMORRAH
Chris Wright
ISBN 1-872410-22-7
292 pages   paperback   £12.95

A story that portrays two opposite ways of life and asks the question: which is sustainable?

SCIENCE AND TECHNOLOGY FOR EIGHT BILLION PEOPLE:
Europe's Responsibility
Edited by Peter H. Mettler
Adamantine Studies on the 21st Century, No. 17
ISBN 0-7449-0125-1
333 pages   hardback   £40.00
Published in association with New European Publications. (Available post-free at £19.95 from New European Publications direct.)

Can Europe take the world lead in championing "Science and Technology with a humane agenda"? What are the short, medium, and long-term priorities of such an agenda and how can the global Science & Technology community as a whole best adopt it in order to serve the basic needs and aspirations of the eight billion people who will inhabit the planet by the year 2020?

This book documents and discusses these issues, as raised at the "Europrospective III" conference in Wiesbaden in 1993.